D0388296

2002 WAYS TO FIND, ATTRACT, AND KEEP A MATE

**Other titles by
Cyndi Haynes and Dale Edwards**

2002 Things to Do on a Date

2002 Ways to Say "I Love You"

2002 WAYS TO FIND, ATTRACT, AND KEEP A MATE

Cyndi Haynes
and Dale Edwards

ADAMS MEDIA CORPORATION
Holbrook, Massachusetts

Acknowledgments

We wish to thank Bob Adams for believing in our books.

We appreciate all the suggestions and assistance on this book from Edward Walters, Mark Maguire, and Rick Dey, whose editorial touches are evident throughout.

A special thanks to Bonnie, Marme, and Bubba, who made our time working on the book so much more fun.

Finally, we send our heartfelt gratitude to Fritzie and "The Boss" for their support and encouragement every step of the way. You two are the very best.

Published by Adams Media Corporation
260 Center Street, Holbrook, MA 02343

ISBN: 1-55850-555-5

Printed in Canada.

J I H G F E D C

Library of Congress Cataloging-in-Publication Data
Haynes, Cyndi.
2002 ways to find, attract, and keep a mate / Cyndi Haynes and Dale Edwards.
p.   cm.
ISBN 1-55850-555-5
1. Mate selection—Miscellanea. 2. Dating (Social customs)—Miscellanea.
3. Single people—Miscellanea. 4. Man-woman relationships—Miscellanea.
I. Edwards, Dale. II. Title.
HQ801.H377   1996
646.7'7—dc20   95-46604
                     CIP

*This book is available at quantity discounts for bulk purchases.
For information, call 1-800-872-5627 (in Massachusetts 617-767-8100).*

Visit our home page at http://www.adamsmedia.com

for W. B. H.

a wonderful man to spend the rest of your life with

Love is not our choice, but in our fate.
—*JOHN DRYDEN*

1. Learn to love yourself first, before trying to find a mate.

2. Know that real love cannot be bought; it can only be found.

3. Dare to be different—you will get noticed.

4. Take full responsibility for your social life.

5. Concentrate on finding Mr./Miss Right at work, as well as working on your career. Treat each "job" equally.

6. While at church, keep your eyes peeled for single people in nearby pews.

7. Shop around for the love of your life at the supermarket. Spend most of your time in the produce section, where people take the longest to pick out their food.

8. If you enjoy being at a bar on the weekends, keep in mind that bars are a great place to meet up with available single people.

9. Sign up for an adult education class at a local college, but don't keep your head buried in the books.

10. When you attend a concert, make friends with all of your seatmates.

11. At the next wedding you attend, get introduced to all the single friends of the bride and groom.

12. Attend singles' dances even if you aren't a great dancer.

13. Spend a lot of free time with friends of the opposite sex. You never know whom you will meet through them.

14. Become friends with your friends' boyfriends and girlfriends; they may know other singles and introduce you to them in the near future.

15. Always look for ways to expand your circle of friends.

16. Teach an adult Sunday school class and tutor any singles in the class.

17. Lounge by the pool during the summer months. Behind your cool sunglasses, keep your eyes wide open for available singles.

18. Get into the swing of things by looking for love on the golf course.

19. Play your own game of love on the tennis court.

20. Enroll in summer school and mingle with the other students after class.

21. Browse for more than just clothes in the men's or women's department of a large department store.

22. Spend a rainy afternoon at a museum hunting for your own kind of treasure—a date.

23. When you need to do laundry, head to a laundromat that is located in an area where a lot of singles live. Go on a weekend when it is very busy and maybe you'll find someone to share a load.

24. Move to a condo with a reputation for being a place singles want to live.

25. Attend all kinds of non-credit classes that appeal to members of the opposite sex.

26. Put on your cowboy boots and take up country line dancing. You might meet the cowboy or cowgirl of your dreams.

27. Make friends with all of your neighbors. Someone could be single or have a friend who is.

28. Throw a great party for all your grade school friends and be extra nice to the single ones.

29. Even if you don't want to, attend all of your high school reunions.

30. Join a ski club and look for love on the snowy slopes.

31. Attend a large bingo match. You might hit a jackpot of a different kind.

32. Stay current on upcoming singles' events in your city.

33. Get a dog (borrow one if you have to) and walk it often.

34. Get your mom to set you up with her friends' children if you don't have someone special in your life right now. Moms love to help with their children's love lives.

35. Host a large cocktail party before your next college reunion and mingle with all of your single classmates.

36. Check up on your old flame. The two of you might be able to work things out and have the greatest love affair of all time!

37. Attend lectures on a variety of subjects (especially those on life in the single lane).

38. When you choose a church to attend, make sure it has a large population of singles.

39. Watch *Oprah* for programs about available singles.

40. Join a popular health club and pump iron after work and on Saturday mornings.

41. Play in a pool tournament and keep your eye on more than the cue ball.

42. Take a self-defense class to meet singles. You might have so many dates after reading this book that you'll have to fight them off!

43. Join a tennis club and spend a lot of time in the lounge visiting with other members.

44. Consider joining a dating service. Check out every one of them in your area. You might just meet somebody special while you are picking up the service's brochure.

45. Become a member of your church's singles' group.

46. Go to investment seminars. You might just meet a wealthy single person.

47. Take a CPR class—you never know when you'll have to save the life of a cute stranger.

48. Join a weeknight bowling league and aim for more than the center pin.

The loving are the daring.
—BAYARD TAYLOR

49. Spend Saturday afternoons with a local bicycle club.

50. Take group dancing lessons, but go without a partner, so you can get fixed up with a great new one.

51. Take your work from the office to the library on the weekends. It is a great place to circulate.

52. Travel with singles' tour groups and keep your eyes on more than the points of interest.

53. Ask your friends to help you meet the love of your life.

54. Attend a variety of sporting events.

55. Look for available single people in your office building.

56. Get your pilot's license and look for singles at airports.

57. Play in a band or sing at a hot night spot.

58. Attend every party that you are invited to.

59. Throw a party at least every other month; be sure to include loads of singles.

60. If you have decided that your date isn't the person of your dreams, discreetly keep your eyes peeled for his friends.

61. Ask your neighbors for a set-up with a great date.

62. Accept all invitations to all events— you never know whom you might meet.

63. If you get called for jury duty, look around at the lawyers, witnesses, and other jurors.

64. Play in a coed volleyball league and serve up some attention to the cute, single members on your team.

65. Invite him to a Sadie Hawkins dance; this gives you a perfect excuse to ask *him* out for a change.

66. Learn the fine art of flirting. It is much easier than you might think.

67. Casually inquire among your co-workers for any possible matches.

68. Get your siblings to set you up with their friends.

69. Read the Sunday paper to look for upcoming events that would be great to take a date to or a good place to meet singles.

70. Work for a large company—the more employees, the more singles.

71. Become pen pals with members of the opposite sex.

72. Get a part-time job in a men's clothing store and give great attention to your single customers.

73. Travel frequently. You never know when and where you might meet your future mate.

74. Apply for a part-time position in a women's shoe store and try to wait on all the single shoppers.

75. Try skydiving—the ratio of men to women is fabulous for women.

76. Attend tournaments at area clubs and mingle with all the spectators.

77. Ask your minister to introduce you to available singles in the congregation.

78. Ask your doctor to fix you up with one of his single patients.

79. If you like the brainy type, join a chess club.

80. Attend trade shows held at hotels and convention centers; these are frequented by singles from all over the country.

81. Stroll through yard and garden shows in the springtime. Singles with a green thumb can be a good bet.

82. Join a coed fantasy sports league and call your fellow members with trades of all kinds.

83. Attend baseball spring training camp and mingle with players and other fans.

84. Go to high school and college football games.

85. Purchase season tickets to basketball games. Instead of staying glued to the game, visit other spectators.

86. At a family reunion, ask if anyone knows of a potential date for you.

87. Look up old friends of the opposite sex.

88. Always attend all functions of any group you belong to. You just might meet someone special.

89. Work for a charity in your community. You might just meet Mr./Miss Right while doing something good for your fellow humans.

90. Go on an all-singles' canoe trip and, while you are paddling along, flirt with any singles who catch your eye.

91. Attend the soccer matches of your children or siblings.

92. Take up white-water rafting for the thrill of it—it's a thrilling way to meet singles!

93. Organize a mixed group to go out once a week to local hot spots.

94. Attend book discussion groups and sit by an attractive single person.

95. Volunteer to help with a political campaign. You might end up married to our next president—or at least another campaign volunteer.

Why not go out on a limb? Isn't that where the fruit is?
—*FRANK SCULLY*

---

96. Rollerblade through crowded parks on the weekends and be on the lookout for the mate of your dreams.

97. Take adult ice skating classes. You might just skate off with a date!

98. Coach a Little League team and look among the spectators for an interesting person to share a hot dog with after the game.

99. Obtain season tickets to a professional football team.

100. Start a home improvement project and ask for help from the good-looking salesperson at the hardware store.

101. Take up fishing—the ratio of men to women is terrific for women.

102. Watch the crowd instead of the pooches at a dog show.

103. Spend Saturday afternoon in the park on a pretty day.

104. Take up jogging in the early-morning hours before you go to work.

105. Borrow a cup of milk from your pretty new neighbor.

106. Stop attractive strangers and ask for change to use in a pay telephone.

107. Attend the openings of the latest blockbuster films.

108. When a new restaurant opens, go there for dinner during the first few weeks when the place is really hopping.

109. Bring in donuts to your office and mingle with your single co-workers.

110. Bake goodies and take them around to your single neighbors.

111. House-sit your friend's condo while he's on vacation and check out his neighbors.

112. Learn the fine art of mingling with strangers. It takes a little practice, but once you get the hang of it, look out, fellow singles!

113. Hang out near the batting cages at parks on the weekends to meet tons of single men of all ages.

114. If you like cowboys and cowgirls, attend rodeos.

115. Chat with other guests while attending a benefit.

116. Check out the other bidders at auctions. You might find someone you are sold on.

117. Always attend your company's Christmas party.

118. If your child's teacher is single, set up an appointment to discuss your child's work. Take an apple to the teacher or ask for a date.

119. Strike up a conversation with people in line with you at the grocery store.

120. Talk to your seatmate when you are on an airplane.

121. Check out all the singles at these big events:

Indianapolis 500	Kentucky Derby
Super Bowl	Olympics
Daytona 500	World Series
U.S. Open	Final Four Games

122. Carpool to work with singles and spend the riding time networking for dates.

123. Ride a different subway or bus route to and from work to look for potential dates.

124. If you like the macho type, be brave and join a motorcycle club.

125. Linger in health food stores and ask cute strangers for advice on what foods to buy.

126. Attend demonstrations at cooking schools to meet singles and learn how to prepare a great meal for your next at-home dinner date.

127. If you like the old-fashioned type of woman, attend county fair bake-offs.

128. To meet young professionals, shop in gourmet food stores.

129. When your pet is sick, take it to a single vet. Let your furry friend be your matchmaker.

130. When buying real estate, give your business to single realtors.

131. Live in the area of your city where singles tend to live.

132. Ride your bicycle through your neighborhood and keep your eyes peeled for interesting newcomers.

133. Go to a single dentist and smile your best smile.

134. Have your will prepared by an unattached lawyer. It could be that the next contract you will need from her is a pre-nuptial agreement for the two of you.

135. When you need to have your teeth cleaned, go to a single dental hygienist.

136. Walk to work and chat with attractive singles along the way.

137. Try hot air ballooning. It is romantic and a sport with a large shortage of women.

138. Roller-skate at local rinks on Saturday afternoons to hunt for your love on wheels.

139. Hire a single accountant to do your tax return. Even if you don't get a refund, you might still end up as a happy taxpayer.

140. Ask your hairstylist for help in setting you up with other clients.

141. Explore your company's phone list for possible dates. Be discreet!

142. If you need to lose weight, check out a Weight Watchers group—you will look better and might meet someone special.

143. While waiting for your car to get serviced at the garage, talk to attractive strangers who are also waiting.

144. Shop for a new car on Saturday afternoons and ask good-looking strangers for their opinions.

145. Buy your life insurance from a single agent and you might soon be purchasing life insurance as a couple.

146. Purchase your car insurance from a single agent.

147. If you like playing pool, spend Saturday afternoons in the local pool halls—the ratio of men to women is great for women.

148. At the next wedding you attend, see if any of the bridesmaids or ushers are single.

149. Go alone to all weddings you are invited to or with a friend of the same sex.

150. Attend auto races and get your love life on track.

151. Participate in community plays. You just might end up starring in your own love story.

152. Everywhere you go, keep your eyes peeled for available singles.

153. Check out your apartment complex for singles.

154. The next time you are visiting your friend's house, ask if there are any singles who are your type living in their neighborhood.

155. Have your hair styled at coed salons.

Help yourself, and Heaven will help you.
—JEAN DE LA FONTAINE

---

156. When you are riding in elevators, scrutinize your fellow riders.

157. Take an art class and check out the work of other artists.

158. Work out at coed gyms and exercise your flirting muscles.

159. Play Frisbee in the park on Saturday afternoons. If you see someone appealing, throw your Frisbee over to her.

160. Attend street fairs on the weekends and mix with the many singles you'll find at these events.

161. Organize a big block party—it's a great way to meet tons of people.

162. Join a Polar Bear club—these mostly male clubs are great for women.

163. Host a benefit for your favorite cause to meet singles.

164. Take an adult education course on a subject that interests you. Many single people attend such courses.

165. Dine alone at seaside restaurants on the weekends, with the hope that a good-looking stranger will cast a net for you.

166. Take part in all church functions and parties.

167. Become a member of your local Welcome Wagon and be sure to greet all the singles who are new to your area.

168. When you have a long train or bus ride to work, strike up a conversation with your seatmate.

169. Make the winning bid at a charity bachelor/bachelorette auction.

170. Participate in a coed card party and maybe you'll be playing the game of Hearts.

171. Take a Dale Carnegie course—you will become more poised among strangers, and you might meet someone special.

172. If you like the sophisticated type, attend art appreciation lectures at trendy galleries.

173. On weekend afternoons, attend movies alone. You might just meet Mr./Miss Right in the lobby.

174. Go to auto shows and check out all the car lovers.

175. Play miniature golf on weeknights during the summer and strike up a conversation with a fellow hacker.

176. Browse through video stores for more than just a movie.

177. Ask a good-looking stranger about a new CD while browsing a music store.

178. Volunteer at a hospital to deliver flowers and gifts to the patients, and be extra friendly to the single ones.

179. Become a tour guide for local points of interest. A charming single may find *you* the main point of interest!

180. Hire an interior decorator who has wonderful community connections and might just introduce you to someone interesting after you have worked together on your home.

181. Sing in a mixed choir. In a little while, you might just be singing songs of love.

182. Meet all your children's friends' parents.

183. Become a member of a sorority or fraternity, where everyone is single and knows tons of other singles.

184. After graduation, become active in the alumni chapter of your fraternity or sorority.

185. Eat breakfast at restaurants in the business district. Ask an intriguing stranger if you can borrow a section of his newspaper.

186. When you eat at fast-food restaurants, eat inside instead of taking the food home. You might meet somebody who is also dining alone.

187. Buy your medicine from single pharmacists—this could be the cure for your lonely heart.

188. Become a lifeguard on the weekends if you like to meet physically active singles.

189. Hang out at winter ski resorts to meet *zillions* of singles.

190. Join the Toastmasters International club to improve your social skills and meet interesting singles.

191. Take an interior design class—this is fabulous for men, as these classes generally have many more women than men.

192. If you are looking for the rowdy type, attend a wrestling match.

193. Work out with an unmarried weight trainer.

194. Purchase your new car from a single salesperson.

195. Visit your parents at their offices to check for any singles working there.

196. Check out your friends' co-workers.

197. If you hear that the new golf pro is single, take some lessons.

198. Ask for gardening tips from the attractive salespeople at your local nursery.

199. Be a scout leader and scan for other parents who are single.

200. Attend all meetings of your professional organization; if you meet any singles, you will at least have something in common with them.

If you cannot inspire a woman with love of you, fill her above the brim with love of herself, and all that runs over will be yours.
—COLTON

---

201. Watch ball games at local parks and mingle among the spectators.

202. Try your luck with the single tennis pro at your club or at a tennis camp.

203. Join the Red Cross—you will help those in need and maybe find the love of your life in the process.

204. Buy several kinds of stock and attend all the stockholder meetings.

205. Bank with unmarried bankers and watch your interest grow.

206. Take a dog obedience class with your pooch to mix with the canine crowd.

207. When you need cash, always go into the bank instead of using ATMs. You might see someone interesting.

208. Ask a single police officer for directions (to his heart).

209. Become a volunteer for Junior Achievement—you will meet parents, other volunteers, and business people in your community.

210. Make some good trades at baseball card shows. Trade your best card for a date.

211. If you are audited by the IRS, find a single accountant.

212. Get involved with your local community theater group.

213. Consider modeling at a large department store on the weekends. You will come in contact with hundreds of people.

214. See if your shrink has a support group for singles.

215. Attend a demolition derby (lots of men and few women).

216. Hire an unattached photographer for your next party or office function.

217. Ask your favorite bartender if he knows of anyone for you to date.

218. Join the Chamber of Commerce and look for singles at the next meeting.

219. Hire a single painter to paint your living room a different color—how about passion pink?

220. Join the Junior League and ask fellow members for help with your love life.

221. Work on a public television auction to catch the eye of other single bidders.

222. Join your neighborhood association. If you don't have one, form one.

223. Stay at bed and breakfast inns when you travel and make friends with the other guests.

224. One of the great things about being single is your freedom. Use it to choose tons of fun activities to meet people.

225. Sit on your porch swing and visit with your single neighbors.

226. Buy season tickets to the symphony and get to know your seatmates.

227. Check out your boss's friends (but be careful).

228. Spend your summer vacation on a dude ranch looking for the right dude.

229. Take a cruise that is for singles only. Be sure to check out the ratio of men to women before you go.

230. Join a hiking club. You can really get to know people while taking a long walk in the beautiful outdoors.

231. If you like the beach bum type, take up surfing.

232. Try fencing—just don't spear the new love of your life.

233. Get involved in a coed ping-pong tournament.

234. Play squash after work and mingle with other players after the game.

235. Take up sailing on the weekends and let the wind steer your heart.

236. Attend hockey games if you like wild and crazy sports fans.

237. Try water-skiing on beautiful summer weekends, and make a splash with other singles.

238. If you want to get into shape and find love at the same time, try taking a coed aerobics class.

239. Take up body building and enter contests with your new physique.

240. Join a croquet league and let the good times roll.

241. Go to polo matches whenever you have the opportunity. You might just meet a prince.

242. Want to mix with a different crowd? Try going to a lacrosse game.

243. If you like the artistic type, take up painting.

244. Try your hand at sculpting and mingle with other artists at shows.

245. Take up bird watching—you never know what will happen while you are waiting in the bushes for that rare bird to come along.

246. Attend film festivals and mix with other moviegoers after the show.

247. Join a garden club or become a judge for their events.

248. Stroll through historic districts on weekends. If you see an attractive stranger, ask questions about the buildings.

249. Attend poetry readings at trendy coffeehouses.

250. Join a preservation society to meet lots of community-minded people.

251. If you are brave, take up hang-gliding (lots of men and very few women).

252. When the weather is pretty, eat outdoors on your lunch hour at little sidewalk cafes or on a bench in a crowded park.

253. Try flying remote-control planes—lots of single dads do this on the weekends.

254. Become a tutor for an adult learning center.

255. Take a computer class in order to re-boot your love life.

256. Become an active member of your college alumni group.

257. Join an exciting travel club that goes to exotic locations.

258. Become a member of an upscale wine-tasting group.

259. Attend the ballet. During intermission, converse with other ballet lovers.

260. Go to the free summer concerts at city parks—there are always tons of singles at these events.

261. When pop and rock stars come to your city, attend the concerts with a group of friends who will be able to introduce you to other people who might also be attending the concert.

262. Become a patron of the opera.

263. Take out a well-written ad in a singles' magazine.

264. If you move to a different city, ask your friends, family, and co-workers for letters of introduction.

265. Check out those closest to you when you are washing your car at a car wash. Always wash your car on a Saturday or Sunday afternoon.

266. If you travel frequently, join the private clubs of the top airlines.

267. Go to a drag race (many more men than women).

It is better to have loved and lost,
than never to have loved at all.
              —ALFRED, LORD TENNYSON

---

268. Spend part of a Saturday afternoon browsing through camera stores.

269. When a new nightclub opens in your city, try to get an invitation to the opening night festivities. That is when the "A List" people will attend.

270. At a stop light, smile and ask the pretty driver in the next car for directions.

271. "Accidentally" crash into a cute stranger's cart in the grocery store.

272. Carry business cards and exchange them with available singles.

273. Volunteer at local museums when large exhibits come to town.

274. Become a member of a yacht club if you like love on the high seas.

275. Spend summer evenings at a beautiful marina scanning for singles.

276. Frequent the bars along the pier (you don't even need to enjoy boating).

277. Walk along the boardwalk on Sunday afternoons and "single watch."

For Single Parents:

278. Join the PTA to look for other single parents—you might even get your kids to help you hunt.

279. Try joining Parents Without Partners to find a new mate.

280. Chaperon school functions and get to know other single parents—maybe you'll end up needing a chaperon of your own!

281. Start a support group for single parents in your area of the city. This can be a great networking system for you.

Not for the Faint-Hearted:

282. Consider joining the National Guard to spend your weekends meeting people from all walks of life.

283. Join the Coast Guard if you have a sense of adventure.

284. If you are strong and brave, consider joining the Marines.

285. Is navy your best color? Then think about joining the Navy!

286. Join the army if you like to get up at the crack of dawn to look for a mate.

287. If you love the beautiful outdoors, consider moving to Alaska.

288. Move to Montana if you'd love to work on a ranch.

(Please note that the above seven suggestions are for women only, as the ratio of men to women is in favor of women.)

289. To make it easy to reach you, have the following:
| Answering machine | Call waiting |
| Call forwarding | Car phone |

290. Never give up hope! It is recorded in *Kentucky Marriages, 1797-1865*, that Moses Alexander, 93, married Mrs. Frances Tompkins, 105, on June 11, 1831.

291. Get a part-time job as a hat check person and mingle with all the single coat owners.

292. If you want to meet a celebrity, enter a "meet the celebrity" contest.

293. Dating fact: Never-married adults account for the largest share of unmarrieds in the United States.

294. Dating fact: 54 percent of all marriages are composed of two never-before-married people.

295. Dating fact: 23 percent of all marriages are remarriages for both the bride and the groom.

296. When you are looking for love, be kind and treat all members of the opposite sex with respect.

297. If you are looking for love and money, you might want to consider moving to one of these states that have the highest personal incomes:

Alaska	California
Connecticut	Illinois
Maryland	Massachusetts
New Hampshire	New Jersey
New York	Washington, D.C.

298. According to the Department of Commerce/Bureau of Census, the median age at a first marriage in the year 1900 was 25.9 for men and 21.9 for women, and more recently 26.5 for men and 24.5 for women. It seems that the more things change, the more they stay the same in matters of the heart.

299. Take an active role in your social life. Don't just sit around and wait for good things to happen. Go out and make them happen!

300. Even if you are the best "catch" in the world, be modest. Nobody wants to listen to a braggart.

301. When you meet a good-looking stranger, be thoughtful and try to make a gesture of kindness that will leave a good impression.

302. Always be sincere and honest, so that you build up a reputation for integrity.

303. Don't panic during a dating dry spell. Everyone goes through those periods when finding the love of your life seems impossible.

304. When you want to create a memorable date, remember that Casanova, (the king of romance), believed chocolate was better than champagne for inducing romantic feelings.

305. It is helpful to know when you are starting to fall for someone special, that men fall in love more quickly than women. Many men fall in love by the end of the fifth date.

306. When considering making a blind date, remember that many couples have had success with this method of dating.

307. The more dates you go on, the more comfortable you will be dating. Practice makes perfect.

308. The average price for a dozen red roses is forty dollars. If that is too expensive for your budget, send a bouquet of mixed flowers instead.

What to Ask When Choosing a Dating Service:

309. Ask for the ratio of men to women. This is very important because many clubs have a shortage of men in certain age groups.

310. Ask what type of reputation the club has. Check with the service for its strengths, but also check with your friends for the real story.

311. Does the club screen members or can anyone join? If they do screen members, how do they do it?

312. Will your last name be given out to other members without your permission?

313. Does the club give out the home telephone numbers of their members?

314. Do they give out members' addresses without written consent?

315. Does the club serve age groups that are compatible with you?

316. Do they offer a trial membership?

317. Can you make monthly payments for the membership fee or do you have to pay up front?

318. What is the club's success rate and what is that based upon?

319. What are their membership requirements?

320. Can you put your membership on hold to pursue a relationship and then come back if the relationship doesn't work out?

321. How many people belong to the club? Can they show you records to prove those figures?

322. How long has the club been in business?

323. What hours are they open?

324. What is expected of their members? Do you have to accept all dates that come your way?

325. You might want to consider getting a job at a dating service instead of joining one. This way you can screen all the members for yourself. The clubs usually have plenty of part-time positions open.

* * *

326. In between dates, spend more time with your friends. This will help keep your spirits up.

327. When your love life isn't going according to your dreams, keep your chin up by doing activities you enjoy.

328. When you answer your telephone, sound pleasant and upbeat. It could be an important love-life call.

329. Before you can get involved in a serious relationship, you need to learn how to give and receive love.

330. It is most important that you learn to distinguish real love from a simple crush that will burn out in a few months.

331. Dating trivia: One out of ten men bring flowers to their dates.

332. If you want help with your love life, just ask—after all, the whole world loves a lover.

333. Always date people who treat you well and make you feel good about yourself.

334. Never leave your house without being well groomed. You will look and feel better.

335. Expect the very best for your love life and take positive steps to make it happen.

336. Make up your own mind about whom to date. Don't let peer pressure set your social calendar.

337. When you need an instant shot of romance, reread your old love letters.

338. Seal a letter romantically by putting SWAK (sealed with a kiss) on it.

339. Go slowly in a relationship where there is a large age difference.

If You Are over Fifty-five, Check Out These Cities
Scottsdale, Arizona
Hot Springs Village, Arkansas
Palm Springs, California
San Diego, California
Boca Raton, Florida
Fort Myers, Florida
Naples, Florida
St. Petersburg, Florida
Maui, Hawaii
Bloomington, Indiana
Carson City, Nevada
Las Cruces, New Mexico
Chapel Hill, North Carolina
Hilton Head, South Carolina
San Antonio, Texas
Hampton, Virginia
Olympia, Washington
Colorado Springs, Colorado

340. Try hiding out in one of these places after a bad date to get your thoughts back together:

Your bedroom	Your bathroom
The rooftop	A fire escape
A child's treehouse	The doghouse (big dog needed)

341. Dating can be stressful because everyone feels the pressure. Try to act in a relaxed manner.

342. As of 1990, there were over fifty million married couples living in the United States. You could be the next one! You just have to keep plugging along in your search for true love.

343. Look for a mate who has the ability to control his or her temper even under the most trying circumstances.

344. Always remember that even the best dates sometimes show their character flaws. Don't panic when your date turns out to be human.

345. If you believe in young love, here's a list of states with the youngest ages for marrying with parental consent and special circumstances:

Alabama—fourteen
Hawaii—fifteen
Massachusetts—fourteen
New Hampshire—thirteen
Texas—fourteen

*Save a boyfriend for a rainy day and another,
in case it doesn't rain.*

—MAE WEST

346. Always look for a mate who has a good sense of self-esteem. If she doesn't love herself, she couldn't possibly love you in a healthy manner.

347. Search for someone with integrity. This will help you know that you have someone who can be counted on when the going gets tough.

348. Before you begin a date, check up on any last-minute plans to make sure the date will run smoothly.

349. If you get nervous about going out, reduce your caffeine intake the day before and day of a date.

350. Use the Internet to find true love.

351. Infatuation is an immediate and strong reaction to another person.

352. There are three characteristics that make for a classy mate:
Confidence
Impeccable manners
A sense of personal style

353. Dating trivia: Almost two-thirds of all first dates end in a kiss.

354. Watch out for singles looking for a transitional relationship (a relationship that is the bridge between the heartache of the last one and the quality one he hopes to have, once he gets over the last break-up). You will only get hurt.

355. Careers that are voted most exciting for making a great first impression:

Actor	Rock star
Senator	Model
Tennis pro	Race car driver
Private investigator	Foreign correspondent
TV reporter	International airline pilot

356. Telephone manners dictate that when you first start calling your new love interest, you call after 9:00 A.M. and before 10:00 P.M.

357. One of the biggest killers of romance is falling into a boring routine.

358. Never assume that everyone who flirts with you is going to ask you out. Many people enjoy flirting simply for the sake of getting attention from members of the opposite sex.

359. Eliminate these items from your dating wardrobe:
Tight clothing
Jewelry that makes a noise when you move
Polyester clothing
Sloppy styles of clothing
Jeans with holes in them
Plunging necklines
See-through blouses

360. Is it real love? Time will tell.

Anastophobia—the fear of kissing

---

361. Even though it can be great fun to gossip about your dates, don't do it because other potential dates will assume you would gossip about *them*.

362. Develop a good sense of humor so that you can enjoy the funny differences between the sexes.

363. Practice being a good listener. Everyone needs someone they can talk to and share confidences with.

364. Give lots of compliments to your friends of the opposite sex, so that you'll feel comfortable complimenting your dates. Everyone likes to hear good things about themselves.

365. Develop resilience to the inevitable rejections that will come your way.

366. Keep your life so full that temporarily not dating will not be a catastrophe for you.

367. Learn to enjoy dating by not taking it so seriously. After all, there are worse things in the world than not having a date or having a bad date.

368. Realize that you don't have to be part of a couple to feel complete. The happier you are on your own, the more attractive you will be to prospective dates.

369. This is an easy rule to follow and it is one of the most important pieces of advice we can give you: *Never* take your date for granted.

370. The five most popular dates in the United States are:
Dinner   Movie
Concert   Spending an evening with
Dancing   friends

371. Always treat your date as you would want to be treated.

372. If you are on a tight budget but still want to serve a nice wine to your date, try an American cabernet sauvignon.

373. You might want to get your single friends together and take out a group personal ad. This can be a lot of fun and you will meet more people this way. Plus, there is safety in numbers.

374. If you and your friends take out a group personal ad, try throwing a party (not at your homes) for the singles who answered the ad and sounded promising.

375. Leave the trauma and stories of your past love relationships out of your conversation on first dates.

376. Keep a first date short so that, if it doesn't work out, you will be glad you didn't waste an entire evening.

377. Dating trivia: Men are more frightened of blind dates than women are.

378. Dating trivia: Men average ten responses from a well-written personal ad.

379. Dating trivia: Women average thirty responses from a well-written personal ad.

380. Keep track of all your dates on a calendar to avoid embarrassing slip-ups.

381. Be brief when you are turning down someone for a date. Don't ramble on and on trying to let him down easily, because he will know exactly what you are up to and feel worse.

382. Even though you might be tempted to forge a romance with a recently divorced person, stop short at friendship. The newly divorced person has many issues to resolve before he can get back out into the dating world.

383. Consider your current love interest's likes and dislikes when you plan a date.

384. When someone asks you out, thank him for the invitation, even if you don't accept.

385. Relationships need commitment, work, and compatibility.

386. Learn to enjoy being alone, so that you don't come across as needy and dependent.

387. When you get dressed for a date, take pride in how you look.

388. Never cancel a date without a valid reason.

389. Real love makes you a better person.

390. Make a detailed list of the qualities you are looking for in a mate, so that you will know you've found the right person when he or she comes along.

391. Androphobia—the fear of men. If you have it, get rid of it before you start dating.

392. If you want to meet a celebrity, join a fan club and attend the meetings the celebrity attends.

393. Keep in mind that no matter how young or old you are, mothers are often wonderful advisors when it comes to your love life.

394. When a date gives you a gift, write a thank-you note and mail it within the week.

395. When you are having a dating dry spell, use the extra time to work on self-improvement, so that when you do meet someone special, you will be ready to dazzle.

396. Always accept a blind date. You might meet someone to fall in love with, or you might make a great new friend.

397. The most popular date activity in the world is going out for dinner.

398. Make a first date short and if it goes well, you can always make a long second date.

399. Stock up on small hostess gifts so that you will always be a welcome guest.

400. Stay away from people who are separated from their spouses. They are still married!

We shall never have friends,
if we expect to find them without faults.
                                        —THOMAS FULLER

---

401. Never tell a date you are dying to get married because it will scare him off!

402. If you aren't dating anyone, spend time with your family and just enjoy being around people who care about you.

403. When planning a date, keep in mind the normal progression of dates:

Coffee/ Drink	Saturday brunch/Weekday lunch
Dinner during the week	Sunday dinner
Saturday night date	Breakfast

404. If you meet a date through a personal ad, provide your own transportation, so that you won't have to rely on a total stranger to take you home.

405. Walk everywhere you go. It gets you into great shape and you might just meet someone along the way.

406. For quick appearance fixers, try a dash of water on your face, eye drops on tired eyes, or bronzing gel.

407. If you meet a cute stranger and can't think of anything to say, talk about world events that are front-page news.

408. Don't talk about the size of your personal income on a date. It isn't anyone's business.

409. Men want a woman whom they think is sexy.

How to Tell if Your Love Interest Is on the Rebound:

410. He talks frequently about his ex.

411. He recently ended a long-term relationship.

412. He doesn't listen to your troubles, but talks about his all the time.

413. He admits he isn't ready for a serious relationship.

414. He doesn't introduce you to all his friends.

415. He doesn't have you around his friends very often.

416. He doesn't talk about the relationship the two of you share in terms of a future.

417. He is often moody, withdrawn, or bitter about love.

418. He is vague about his feelings for you.

419. He doesn't invest emotionally in your relationship.

The Ten Best Occupations for Meeting People from All Backgrounds:
Doctors
Journalists
Tour Guides
Police Officers
Realtors
Flight Attendants
Hairstylists
Florists
Retail Salespeople
Car Salespeople

420. Take a vacation at a singles-oriented resort, such as Club Med.

421. Pretend to take a survey, say, on eating habits or media preferences, and question every single in sight.

422. If you are feeling nervous about asking someone out on a date, have a friend check out that person's feelings about you before extending the invitation.

423. If you aren't dating anyone, you probably have a lot of free time. Put that time to good use by hunting harder for someone to date.

424. One of the reasons that blind dates work out is that the person you are being set up with has already met with approval from the friend or relative who arranged the date.

425. Many people claim they are too set in their ways to get out and date. This is a common excuse used by older singles. Don't fall into this rut!

426. Everyone likes a compliment, so if you are thinking good things about a handsome stranger, pass them on. It could be the beginning of a great love affair.

427. Men are slower to make commitments than women. If you are a woman, learn to take things slowly.

428. Women should also keep in mind that the number one complaint from men about women is that women are too possessive.

429. Most people can be charming for a few hours, but it is much harder to carry on a conversation for hours on end. Keep early dates short.

430. Most women want to become mothers, so they look at their dates as potential fathers of their children.

431. When you turn down a date, be polite and kind. Nobody likes being turned down.

432. Men and women are both looking for a mate who is fun to be around. Get rid of your gloom-and-doom attitude.

433. Never, ever date someone who is married!

434. Dating trivia: The first Hershey kiss was introduced in 1907; the candy is now produced at a rate of twenty million a day.

435. If you give a dating ultimatum, be sure to carry it out. Never make idle threats.

436. Men look for attractiveness first, while women look first for confidence and competence.

437. Singles are attracted to those who make them feel good about themselves.

438. If you live in an apartment complex, constantly be on the lookout for new singles, as people move in and out all of the time.

439. Look into having plastic surgery if you feel you have a serious flaw in your appearance.

440. Before you go on a date, make sure the clothes you are wearing fit properly.

441. Visit an image consultant to learn how to appear more confident and in control. This will help with both your love life and your career.

442. Wear fashionable clothes that are well suited to you. Develop your own sense of style.

443. Look closely at the person you want to date and ask yourself if you would want a friend or sibling to date this person. If not, move on.

444. Most love triangles are "wrecktangles."

445. The best rule for dressing for a special date is to plan ahead.

446. Wear clothes that highlight your personality.

447. Speak well! Slang terms to drop from your vocabulary:
"Ya" for you
"Ain't" for are not
"Dunno" for do not know
"Gonna" for going to
"Huh" for excuse me

448. Research suggests that women are attracted to men who wear red ties or sweaters.

449. A good rule of thumb to follow when getting dressed for a date is that it is better to be underdressed than overdressed.

450. A great way to meet other single people is to host a singles' party and invite your single friends to bring their single friends.

451. Flirt: The girl who got the boy *you* wanted.

452. Flirtation: The art of gaining attention without intention.

453. It is simply not true that nice guys are wimps and therefore aren't any fun to date.

Reasons Why Weddings Are Great Places to Meet That Special Someone:

454. Everyone is in a festive and romantic mood.

455. Your friends are there for support.

456. You are dressed up and looking your best.

457. You can scan for singles during the ceremony.

458. You can mingle at the reception.

459. You have something in common with every person at the wedding—you know the bride and groom.

460. You can get your friends to introduce you to singles you don't know at the reception.

461. Your friends can keep the conversation going with an attractive stranger until you feel comfortable on your own.

462. You can ask people to dance without feeling self-conscious.

463. You might catch the bridal bouquet and change your luck!

* * *

464. If you are feeling stressed before a big date and have a headache, take two aspirin with a cup of coffee or a Coke.

465. On dates, relax and make light of any klutzy moves on your part.

466. Even if you think your date is paying for the date, carry money just to be on the safe side.

467. On most dates, the person who does the asking out pays for the cost of the date.

468. Never agree to go on a date if the only reason you are going is to avoid hurting someone's feelings.

469. Even if you aren't the one in charge of planning the date, have a back-up plan in case the first set of plans fall through.

470. Drop your love interest if she is hypercritical. Everyone has faults, but if you feel like you are receiving too much criticism, find someone who appreciates you.

471. Hunt for a significant other who is mature enough to handle a long-term commitment.

472. If you realize that your love interest isn't the one for you, move on. If you stay in a dead-end relationship, you will be wasting valuable time that you could put to better use by hunting for a new love.

473. Love can make your whole life brighter!

474. A bad date is a lot like an appendix: You can take him out, but once is enough!

475. Before you get involved in an office romance, consider:
What will happen to your job if you break up?
Will the office gossip bother you?
Will you need to keep the relationship a secret?

The love you give away is the only love we keep.
—ELBERT HUBBARD

---

476. Most marriages in countries such as Japan and India are still arranged by parents, and the divorce rates are low in these countries. Ask your parents for their opinion of your newest love interest.

477. When you talk to a date, be animated. You want to be fun and upbeat.

478. Never tell a sexist joke.

479. Remove any breathiness from your voice. It isn't the least bit sexy.

480. Love does three important things for humankind. It makes us feel better, look better, and live longer. It may just be exactly what the doctor ordered!

481. When you first fall in love, you will feel very vulnerable. Learn to relax and just go with your feelings instead of trying to run from your fears. Eventually, you will feel more secure.

482. Rivalry can ruin the best of romances. Learn to think of you and your date as a team, not as competitors.

483. Flirting should always put the other person at ease while adding a sense of excitement to the conversation.

484. The key components of good flirting are recognizing that the two of you are members of the opposite sex and enjoying the differences.

485. Keep your jokes current. There is nothing funny about a stale joke.

486. Out of respect, men should always stand when their date enters the room.

487. Before you go on a date, say a prayer.

488. To help you relax while getting dressed for a big date, play soothing music.

489. Try to have a date on holidays. This helps make special occasions even more memorable.

490. Remind yourself of all the reasons why someone would want to date you.

491. Before you go out looking for love, listen to upbeat music that puts you in a brave, bold frame of mind.

492. If you need to improve your fashion sense, read:

Glamour	*GQ*
Vogue	*Seventeen*
Harper's Bazaar	*Mademoiselle*

493. Love is the best reason of all for wanting to get married.

494. Love accepts imperfections and differences between two people.

495. If you have to talk about your past loves, call a friend; don't tell a date about your dating history until the relationship is serious.

496. Don't try too hard to please your date. Nobody wants a "yes" man. Just be yourself and have fun.

497. Some singles are afraid of marriage because of feelings of sexual inadequacy. If this is your situation, seek help from a competent psychologist.

498. Even if you feel nervous on a date, keep your body still. Don't be jumpy or you will make your date feel uncomfortable.

499. Dating trivia: Nearly 25 percent of women pay their own way on a date.

500. Some singles are simply looking for someone to take out for a specific occasion such as their company Christmas party. They are not looking for a marriage partner. Learn to spot these people if your priorities differ.

501. Some younger singles, especially those in their early twenties, are only looking for a casual relationship.

502. However, the majority of singles as a group are looking for a serious relationship that will eventually lead to marriage.

503. Gestures of romance:

Caress	Embrace
Kiss	Hold
Cuddle	Hug
Snuggle	Pamper

Can you name another?

504. Get involved in a loving relationship so that you can share your joys and sorrows.

505. Learn to take risks in matters of the heart.

506. If you are worried about being rejected, ask yourself, "Can I survive the rejection?" If the answer is "yes," then forget the worry and go forward.

507. If your date doesn't like you, life will still go on. Lighten up!

508. Before approaching a new love interest, visualize a successful romance.

509. Never trust a date who says, "Trust me."

510. If you double-date with a married couple, make sure they are happily married. You want to spend time with people who are good marriage role models.

511. Never date people you feel sorry for. You need to respect your dates, not pity them.

512. Our best advice on pick-up lines? Be sincere or really fun and outrageous.

513. Line: "Your legs must be tired as you've been running through my mind."

514. Line: "Who stole the moonlight and put it in your eyes?"

515. Line: "You might just be the love of my life."

516. The most overused pick-up line: "What's your sign?"

517. One of the most popular pick-up lines: "Do you have the time?"

518. If you want to catch the eyes of singles, try walking down the street with a beautiful Afghan hound at your side.

519. Ask a good-looking stranger:
To carry your groceries or help with a big box
To hold open a door when your arms are full

520. Be cautious when you date people who have a bad track record in love. If your new love interest has a history of broken relationships, you can be sure there is a good chance that your heart will get broken.

521. Read love poetry at night under the stars.

522. If you want to feel romantic, wear silk and lace, instead of denim and leather.

523. Savor the early days of a new relationship—someday these will be the "good old days."

Dating Definitions:

524. Charm—the ability to make someone else think both of you are pretty wonderful.

525. Bachelor—a man who tries to avoid the issue.

526. Checkmate—the person you marry for money.

* * *

527. Touch your date lightly to show your romantic interest in him.

528. When you see your love interest from a distance, wave to get his attention and show how glad you are to see him.

529. If you are involved in a healthy relationship, you will have a deep sense of caring between the two of you.

530. Invite a date over to watch a special television program when you don't feel like going out on the town.

531. You need to know how to manage your feelings so you don't overwhelm your love interest.

How Do You Really Feel about Your Current Dating Interest?

532. Do I respect her as a friend and a possible marriage partner?

533. Do I genuinely like her?

534. Would I want to grow old with this person?

535. Does the future look brighter with this person in it?

536. Is she really what I'm looking for or am I settling because I'm lonely?

537. Would I want her to be the other parent of my child?

* * *

Sympathetic Listeners about Your Love Life (for Men):
Best Friend
Sisters
Friends
Aunts
Brothers
Roommates
Co-workers
Grandmothers

538. Don't tell a new love interest that sometimes you still date your ex just because you haven't met anyone else.

539. If you need to turn down a date, but you don't want to hurt his feelings, just tell him you are currently involved in a serious relationship.

540. After a break-up, be kind regarding your ex so you don't unintentionally fuel rumors.

Gallantry consists of saying the most empty things
in an agreeable manner.
—DUC FRANÇOIS DE LA ROCHEFOUCAULD

541. In a healthy relationship, partners are treated equally.

542. Get plenty of sleep the night before a big date.

543. Give your significant other an old-fashioned ID bracelet engraved with a romantic message inside.

544. Plan small surprises for your dates to make them exciting.

Tips for Finding Long-Lost Loves:

545. Call your old flame at the last known telephone number. If she no longer lives there, ask the person who answers if he has a current number or address.

546. Call her parents and ask for her current address.

547. Ask her friends for her telephone number.

548. Check with her employer for her work telephone number.

549. If you went to school together, contact the chairman of the reunion committee to get her address.

550. Search through wedding announcements and hope you don't find her name!

551. Call telephone information to see if she left a forwarding telephone number.

552. Place an ad in newspapers requesting information about her current whereabouts.

553. Ask at all her old hangouts if anyone knows anything that might help you find her.

554. Check with her other old flames to see if they have an address.

555. If you are really serious about finding her, hire a private investigator.

556. Don't give up if you believe that she is the one for you.

557. If all else fails, contact the television show, *Unsolved Mysteries*.

* * *

558. Try a part-time job as a waitperson—a great way to meet all kinds of people!

559. Follow your heart, but listen to your head too.

560. If possible, try out living in different parts of the country— if you don't find a mate in one town, you might in another.

561. It's not true that men aren't attracted to women who wear glasses. But if you do wear them, make sure they are flattering to your features.

562. If you see a cute stranger and can't think of anything to say, talk about the weather if it has been unusual or extremely nice.

563. If you have any skeletons in your closet, keep them there.

564. Always leave your dates wanting more.

565. You will feel more pressure if you plan a long first date, so plan a date that lasts two hours or less.

566. A women looks for a man who dresses well, so she will be proud to be seen with him.

567. The newly widowed are singles you can be friends with, but it is best not to date them because they need time to work through their grief.

568. Beware: Dating ultimatums can backfire!

569. If you have a date directly after work, take these items to the office:

Jewelry	Evening make-up
Perfume	Evening handbag
Dress shoes	Money

570. If your teeth need to be straightened, get braces.

571. Wear clothes in colors that are flattering to you.

572. When getting dressed for a date, make sure your clothes fit your self-image.

573. An invitation with R.S.V.P. on it tells you to let the hostess/host know if you will be attending or not.

574. An invitation with "Regrets Only" on it means you should respond only if you can't attend.

575. To be a welcomed guest, always answer all invitations promptly.

576. For the brightest smile:
See your dentist regularly
Have your teeth whitened
Practice smiling in front of a mirror

577. It isn't true that men are only after sex in relationships.

When Asking Someone for a Date:

578. Know what the plans are for the date.

579. Know your budget and what you can comfortably afford to spend.

580. Ask for the date in a confident and upbeat manner.

581. Ask politely; don't give the impression you are doing someone a favor by asking her out.

582. Give a choice of two times or two activities, if at all possible.

583. If the person is busy, suggest an alternate plan.

584. Consider sending an invitation for the date in the mail to make it special.

585. If you don't want to kiss someone goodnight, simply turn your head or step back a little.

586. Relax!

* * *

Sympathetic Listeners about Your Love Life (for Women):
Best Friend
Grandmothers
Fathers
Sisters
Roommates
Aunts
Co-workers (if trustworthy)
Big brothers
Friends (if trustworthy)

587. Don't tell a new love interest that you just got out of a long-term relationship, because it might scare her away.

588. When you write a thank-you note, be sure to express your gratitude for the gift and mention how you will use it in the future.

589. During a dating dry spell, throw yourself into your work so that, when you do need to take time off for a special date, you will be able to because you have put in so much overtime.

590. Just remember it is often the newest key on the ring that opens the door.

591. One of the advantages of a blind date is that if it doesn't work out, the date might be able to introduce you to someone you will like.

592. Consider serving an inexpensive American blush wine to a date if you are on a tight budget.

593. Many singles claim that they want to remain single instead of being tied down by a serious relationship. Don't buy it. They would love to have someone special in their life.

594. The most common names for kissing:

Smooching	Swapping spit
Bundling	Necking
Fooling around	Sucking face
Submarine racing	Making out

Do you have an unusual one?

595. If you have the latest Hollywood gossip, be sure to pass it on to the nearest available single if you want to start an interesting conversation.

596. If you have strong political views, you might want to keep them to yourself on a first date. Save them for a future date, then present them in a non-threatening manner.

597. Keep your heart in the present and not in the future.

Nobody will ever win the battle of the sexes. There's too much fraternizing with the enemy.
—HENRY KISSINGER

---

598. A man wants a date who is smart and whom he considers an equal.

599. If you meet someone who is separated, wait until the divorce is final before you date them.

600. If you have to use an ultimatum, be sure to time the delivery of it for the greatest impact.

601. Only use a dating ultimatum as a very last resort, and only for serious issues.

602. If you want to have a dazzling smile, consider having your teeth capped. Many of Hollywood's biggest stars got their beautiful smiles this way.

603. Visit a health club regularly to get the body of your dreams. This will improve your shape and enhance your self-esteem.

604. Look in your closet and see if your clothes are up-to-date with the fashion trends in your city.

605. Only wear clothes that are appropriate for your age group.

Impress Your Date! Guidelines for Tipping:
Restaurants—15 to 20 percent of the bill
Coat checks—fifty cents to a dollar per item
Taxis—15 to 20 percent of the fare
Headwaiter—five to ten dollars for reserving a special table

---

606. If you regularly park in a parking garage, start parking near a cute single person and strike up a conversation on the way to the elevators.

607. If you dial the wrong number, but like the sound of the voice at the other end of the line, start up a conversation. It might just lead to a date.

608. Pretend to have car trouble and ask a single co-worker for a ride home.

609. For men only: Borrow a friend's baby and head to the park on a pretty afternoon.

610. Make this your *search for love* motto: "Go straight ahead, you can't dodge destiny."

611. Politically correct terms for boyfriends and girlfriends:
Significant other   Partner
Companion   Spouse equivalent

612. Never believe that being nice isn't sexy. Everyone wants someone who treats them like a king or queen.

613. When you buy a fragrance, consider one with a romantic name to get you into a loving frame of mind.

614. Happiness is like a kiss—in order to get any good out of it, you have to give it to somebody else.

615. If you want to get married, you might start a hope chest to store items for the home of your dreams.

616. Research shows that couples who live together before marriage are more likely to divorce than those who don't.

617. If you are afraid of missing an important love-life call, carry a beeper.

618. If you have Call Waiting for your telephone, don't interrupt a call from Mr./Miss Right to take another call. That is too rude for words!

619. Forget about fads when you buy most of your clothing.

620. Avoid status items when getting dressed. Some prospective dates will be impressed, but many will think you are shallow.

621. Avoid taking excessive amounts of cold remedies in the winter. They can be extremely drying to the lips. Nobody wants to kiss cracked, dry lips.

622. Dating rule: Always be nice and play fair.

623. Drop your love interest if he is insensitive to your feelings.

624. If your love interest doesn't look at you often, he is either very shy or just not interested. People in love can't take their eyes off each other.

625. Only date people who are high on life. You need someone to build you up, not bring you down.

626. True love cannot be rushed!

627. When in doubt about kissing a date goodnight, don't.

628. If you kiss a date in public, keep it short. The rest of the world doesn't want to watch.

629. Your electric mixer *and* your oven are powerful romantic tools. Don't forget to bake some goodies for your dates.

630. Many professional matchmakers are quite reasonably priced; but even if their fees seem high, how much is too much for real love?

631. Develop a speaking voice with full, rich tones to make you sound attractive and mature.

632. If you plan to tell your date a joke, practice it on a friend first.

633. Men should always help their date on with a coat. It is a good excuse to put your arm around her.

634. If you are feeling nervous about a date, reduce loud noises around you when you are getting dressed to go out.

635. Practice positive imaging. In your mind's eye, always picture your love life running smoothly.

636. Forget about past bad dates. Dwelling on dating horror stories will only make you nervous about dating.

Develop the Proper Dating Mind-Set:

637. Get strength and wisdom from your spiritual beliefs.

638. Never dwell on the worst-case scenario. Thinking about what can go wrong will only scare you and it won't prevent the worst from happening.

639. Visualize the mate of your dreams. After all, you deserve the very best.

640. Live in the present. You don't want to live in a past relationship, nor waste time worrying about a future one.

641. Don't compare yourself to others.

642. Give yourself time to unwind after work before going out on a date.

643. Be level-headed when you are dating. You need to keep a sense of balance in your love life.

* * *

644. Before you introduce your new love interest to your pet, make sure your date likes animals. During the introduction, be sure to reassure your furry friend.

645. Build a complete life outside of your romantic social life that includes:

Church	Work/career
Education	Friends
Family	Self-improvement
Exercise	Pets
Hobbies	Travel
Community involvement	

646. If you both have to work late at the office, have a fifteen-minute phone date during the course of the evening.

647. If you get sick and can't go out on a date, phone or fax your date.

648. Get a cellular phone so you can phone your date on the road if necessary.

649. If you can't get together because of schedule conflicts, link up your computers for a quick, high-tech date.

650. Try not to call your date by the name of your last love interest. But if you do, don't make a big deal of it.

651. Line: "Your name must be Sugar because you look so sweet."

652. Line: "I've seen you somewhere before. Was it on a magazine cover?"

653. Line: "You must be a thief. You stole the stars from the sky and put them in your eyes."

654. Opposites attract, but they don't always get along.

655. Reenact your best date, even if it is with a new partner.

656. Men react strongly to women who are fussy and hard to please. They dump them.

657. Women don't like it when a man refuses to dress up for any of their dates together.

658. Never compare your date to your ex-love.

659. Be sure to have a nice outfit to wear for brunch or going to church.

660. Go through your closet and get rid of all the stuff that is unflattering or out of style. If you aren't sure about an item, ask a friend.

661. Women want men to be gentlemen. Use good manners and treat her like the lady she is.

662. Some men think it is sexy when a woman plays with her hair while she is talking to him.

663. Tell your date that she looks beautiful or he looks handsome.

664. A mature date will have long-range plans and goals for his life. He will also have a track record of reaching his goals.

665. "You can't judge a book by its cover" means sometimes first impressions are wrong. Think twice before turning down a date.

666. For a successful relationship, build fun and loving memories.

667. Before you leave home to meet your date, look at yourself in a full-length mirror.

668. Give your special someone a friendship ring when you feel your relationship is turning serious.

669. Old-fashioned romance is back in style.

670. Casual sex is a thing of the past for most dating singles.

A Year of Holiday Reasons for Asking Someone Out:

671. A Super Bowl party in January can beat the wintertime blues.

672. Valentine's Day is a great time for a no-date party.

673. Get together for a glass of green beer at an Irish pub on St. Patrick's Day.

674. Dye Easter eggs together for your favorite charity's egg hunt.

675. Watch the Kentucky Derby on your big-screen TV while you drink mint juleps.

676. Make a date to watch the Fourth of July fireworks.

677. A Labor Day picnic at a romantic spot can end the summer on a good note.

678. Bring a special friend to Thanksgiving dinner at your parents' house.

679. Try a tree-trimming party at your place. You can be creative with even the smallest tree!

680. New Year's Day brunch at a fabulous restaurant starts the year off right.

Stand with anybody who stands right,
and part with him when he goes wrong.
—ABRAHAM LINCOLN

---

681. If you have a beach date, treat yourself to a pedicure.

682. Have your hair styled at a quality salon. A good haircut can make a huge difference in your appearance.

683. When deciding what to wear on a date, make sure the outfit is right for your planned activity.

684. It is a common dating misconception that women only look for men with large incomes.

685. The key to finding love is perseverance.

686. The key to having a good relationship is wanting one.

687. Watch out! It is absolutely true that love can be blind.

688. Even though it can be difficult at times, keep your heart open and ready for love.

689. Refuse to pour your emotions into a relationship that doesn't meet your emotional needs.

690. Do you want some encouraging love-life news? The United States has one of the highest percentages of marriages in the world.

691. Is he teasing you? Then you know he is interested.

692. Men don't focus on conversation in the same way that women do. Men are action oriented, while women aren't.

693. If you notice that she is often in close proximity to you, then she probably likes you.

694. Choose simple, clean lines in your clothing styles.

695. If you want to have luck at work finding love, keep a tidy office or work space. First impressions are important!

696. If you get chapped lips, soothe them with an over-the-counter antibiotic treatment.

697. Even the worst dates only last for several hours. You can endure!

698. Your age should not be an issue when deciding whether to get serious with someone. If you haven't met the right mate, don't get married; if you have, do!

699. Wealth and power are wonderful things, but don't let them blind you when you are looking for love.

700. Dump your new love interest if she cheats on you. If she did it once, she will probably do it again. Why wait around to find out?

701. If your love interest uses "closed" body language when he is near you, he probably isn't interested in you.

702. On a bad date, either grin and bear it or ask to go home.

703. Sometimes looking for love feels like looking for a job. You hunt for a prospect, you interview, you market yourself, and you keep at it until you find what you are looking for.

Ways to Win Back an Old Flame:

704. Remain calm! Many couples get back together after a break-up.

705. Take things slowly. If you rush things, you just might scare your old flame and cause him to back away.

706. Develop other interests besides your ex.

707. Keep in touch with your ex on a regular basis.

708. Let your ex know how you feel.

709. If you want to play just one game, make him a little jealous. Don't let him think that you are just sitting around waiting for him to come back to you.

710. Stop yourself from putting too many demands on your ex.

711. Become friends again before moving back into a dating relationship.

712. Talk about the happy times you shared together.

713. Visualize getting back together every morning before you get out of bed.

* * *

Faithfulness is one of the marks of genius.
—CHARLES BAUDELAIRE

714. Get on the mailing lists of art galleries, concerts, auctions, benefits, and any other events in your area that you could attend to meet singles.

715. Adopt a dating "godmother" (someone who will take an interest in your love life and give you good, sound advice).

716. Never kiss and tell. This is a lesson you should have learned back in grade school.

717. If you feel that your dating patterns are self-destructive, ask a trusted friend for her advice. If this doesn't help, you might want to seek advice from a professional.

718. Create a sense of warmth and compassion through your voice. This will encourage dates to confide in you.

719. When a couple is getting into a car, the man should open the door for the woman.

720. He should do the same when they are getting out of the car. To be proper, he should walk behind the car when going around to open her door, not in front.

721. Call your date to confirm the time you are going out if you made plans a week or two in advance.

722. Choose your dates wisely. People judge you by the company you keep.

723. If you flirt on a date, make sure that it is with your date and not with other people.

724. It is always great to have a Saturday night date since this night is commonly known as "date night."

725. If you are feeling nervous about a date, just remember that in a few short hours you will be back home with (hopefully) some wonderful memories.

726. Take a friend along when you are searching for someone special to date. This will make it more fun and your friend can help keep your spirits up.

727. You aren't alone in your search for Mr./Miss Right. There are millions of single people just like you looking for love.

728. Try to give up smoking because most people don't like to kiss someone with smoker's breath.

729. Many people want to get married to have a sense of security. It is nice to know that you are always going to have one special person you can count on.

730. Love always begins with respect.

731. Sexist remarks are one of the biggest dating turn-offs. This is the 1990s, not the 1950s.

732. When you walk into a room, hold your head up high.

733. Tilt your upper torso toward your date, to suggest that you are hanging on her every word.

Good Conversation Tips:

734. Maintain eye contact throughout the entire conversation.

735. Smile often.

736. Nod your head in agreement with what your date has to say.

737. Listen intently. You want to learn as much as you can, so you can decide if this is the person for you.

738. Ask lots of questions, but don't interrogate.

739. Be sincere and natural.

740. Don't fidget or you will distract your date's attention from the conversation.

741. Use your sense of humor to keep things fun and lively.

742. Show a genuine interest in your date's opinions.

743. Be modest. You want to shine, not show off.

744. Form a positive image by only saying good things about yourself.

745. Keep the flow of conversation going by talking about lots of different topics.

746. Have a good command of the language. You want to be able to tell your date exactly how you feel.

747. Learn to change topics easily, so you don't have to talk about subjects you would rather not talk about.

748. Practice speaking with good diction. Dates will judge you on how you sound.

749. Work constantly on increasing your vocabulary.

750. Be sensitive. Avoid topics that might make your date feel uncomfortable.

751. Show respect for your date's ideas, even if you don't agree with them.

752. Even if you are nervous, maintain clarity of thought.

* * *

753. Trust your significant other if he tells you that you deserve better than him. After all, he should know.

754. The world was made for couples, so keep looking till you find the love of your life.

755. Know that rejection is a part of the dating scene. It happens to everybody at one time or another.

756. Stay away from dates who want to borrow money from you. You don't need to pay someone to date you.

757. Study your friends' love lives for clues on successful dating behavior.

758. Ask a good-looking stranger if you can borrow a pen when you are standing in line at a bank.

759. If you want to look chic, walk a Doberman.

760. Many singles continue to date someone even if they know that it won't lead to marriage because they feel comfortable in the relationship and are scared of the unknown.

761. At the movies, watch romantic love stories instead of action blockbusters.

762. Wear a great-smelling fragrance that lightly lingers in the air. Spray it on your love letters.

763. Work at being a person who laughs a lot. Everyone wants to be around someone who is fun and having a good time.

764. In a good relationship, both partners respect each other.

765. Use an answering machine to screen your calls.

766. You need to balance a relationship with the rest of your life and not make it a reason for living.

767. Take full responsibility for the quality of your life. Don't make excuses or blame others.

768. Treat yourself with dignity; otherwise, you won't get the respect you deserve.

769. Learn to accept your flaws. You are only human.

The first ingredient in conversation is truth, the next good sense, the third, good humor, and the fourth, wit.
—SIR WILLIAM TEMPLE

---

770. The average cost for a half-carat diamond engagement ring is $9506.

771. Send a box of chocolates to your love interest with a note saying you are sweet on him.

772. Never, ever confuse sex with intimacy.

773. Are you scared to date? Do it anyway! You'll be glad you did.

774. Before you leave to pick up your date, make sure you have the correct address.

775. Never make a promise that you don't intend to keep.

776. To make a good impression, always be on time.

Are You Good Dating Material?
Ask Yourself the Following Questions:

777. Is my attitude positive?

778. Am I physically fit or do I need to lose weight?

779. Are my clothes stylish enough or do I need to buy a few things?

780. Am I willing to try new things?

781. Am I willing to meet new people?

782. Do I have good grooming habits?

783. Would I want to date someone like myself?

784. How can I improve myself to be more attractive to members of the opposite sex?

785. Am I over all past relationships?

* * *

786. Are you looking for a college-educated mate? These are the states with the highest percentages of people with bachelor's degrees:

California	Pennsylvania
New York	Texas
New Jersey	Ohio
Florida	Massachusetts
Illinois	Michigan

787. Nice people are just as passionate as those who are cocky and arrogant.

788. If you look up and find someone staring at you, he might just be interested in you.

789. Be sure to keep your hairstyle simple, current, and in keeping with the styles of clothes you wear.

790. If you are on a tight budget, keep in mind that traditional clothes stay in style longer than trendy clothes.

791. While on vacation, guard against singles who are just looking for a fling and not for a long-term relationship. Don't settle for anything less than a total commitment.

792. Stop a cold sore with a water-soluble, 2 percent solution of zinc salts if you feel a sore popping up before a big date.

793. Drop your love interest if she flirts with others in front of you. You want to be your love's one and only.

794. If you feel like you are falling in love, check for these symptoms:

Chills	Lightheartedness
Sighing	Pounding heart
Jelly legs	Trouble concentrating
Trembling	Butterflies in your tummy

795. If you are sick, don't you dare kiss your date goodnight.

796. More and more singles are turning to professional matchmakers, because they don't have a lot of free time to look for love. An expert does the legwork for them. Have you tried one?

797. Talk to your date in your normal speaking voice. Don't be affected.

798. If you take your date to an elegant restaurant, offer to order for her.

799. Learn to meditate to calm your nerves before an important date.

800. Before going out on a long date, take a twenty-minute nap to give yourself an extra burst of energy.

801. Get a professional manicure. Hands are one of the first things many people notice about a prospective date.

802. Ask a fashion consultant for advice about your wardrobe. Many department stores have consultants and their services are free just for shopping at that particular store.

803. Stay current on world events, the world of entertainment, local news, and trendy hot topics so you will be a great conversationalist.

804. Develop lots of interests, so you will have many different ways to meet people.

805. If she flirts with you in front of her friends, she is probably very interested. Go after her!

806. Drop your current flame if he ignores you when someone or something more important comes along.

Create Your Own Dating Goals:
Number of People Per Week You Plan To:
Flirt with _____
Send a fun greeting card to _____
Say hello to _____
Telephone for a quick visit _____
Fax a message to _____
Meet _____
Ask out for a date _____

807. Throw a BYOB/BYOG (bring your old boyfriend/ girlfriend) party for a very interesting way to meet other singles. This makes for a unique evening and you will hear some great stories about your friends.

808. Stop yourself from telling a "dirty" joke on a date, no matter how funny you think it is.

809. Before a big date, leave a little extra time for an unexpected emergency.

Dating Tips for Single Parents:

810. Tell your children how to reach you and what to do in various emergency situations while you are out.

811. Realize that the dating scene has changed since you were out there.

812. Ask your friends for support and advice.

813. Don't rush yourself into dating, no matter what your friends say.

814. Don't allow your children to stop you from dating. Many kids are jealous of a new love interest at first, but they get over it.

815. Never let your children tell you whom you can and can't date. It is your love life and you need to make the decisions.

816. Talk to your children about your reentry into the dating world.

817. Expect some resistance at times from your children about your love life.

818. Don't allow your ex to tell you whom you can date.

819. Don't let a tight budget keep you from dating. Plan less expensive activities.

820. Balance your children's needs with your social life.

821. Work through your anger with your ex before you start dating again.

822. Don't be jealous of your children's love lives if theirs are going better than yours.

823. Be a dating role model for your children.

824. Learn to enjoy your own company before your start dating again.

825. Realize that dating may be frightening at first, but after a few dates, you'll be back into the swing of things.

826. Don't rush into another marriage!

* * *

To love and win is the best thing: to love and lose the next best.
—WILLIAM M. THACKERAY

How to Introduce Your Children to Your Date:

827. Tell your children about your "new friend" before you introduce them.

828. Make the introduction casual, not a major production.

829. Make their initial time together short and sweet.

830. Don't push either party to form a grand friendship. Let things unfold naturally.

831. Help your children to feel comfortable with your new relationship. Reassure them that you care about them as much as ever.

832. After the initial meeting, talk to your children and ask them for their impressions.

833. Keep an open channel of communication with your kids.

834. Be sure to introduce your children to your "new friend" before someone else does. You want your kids to hear about your love life from you.

Osculation—the act of kissing
Philematology—the study of kissing

---

835. Women are looking for men who have a good sense of humor and a sense of fun about life.

836. If you have to turn a date down, be firm. Don't let yourself be talked into going on a date you don't want to go on.

837. Men are looking for women who are kind and tender-hearted.

838. When you double date, only double with couples who are fun and not fighting with each other all the time.

839. You can tell if someone is interested in you if he makes up excuses to talk with you. Don't be surprised if you get asked the same questions again and again.

840. Don't let your search for true love take over your entire life. Learn to integrate it gracefully into the other aspects of your life.

How to Make a Great First Impression
When Meeting Your Date's Children:

841. Learn a little bit about the kids before you meet them.

842. Meet on neutral territory, instead of at their home. That way they won't feel like you are invading their space.

843. Refrain from making a negative comment about their other parent (wear a muzzle if you need to).

844. Be casual. Don't turn this first meeting into a big deal.

845. Consider bringing a small gift. Ask your date for suggestions.

846. Be friendly even if the child is cool to you. You are the adult—act like one!

847. Be yourself. Kids can sense a phony a mile away.

848. Don't try too hard to please the children. You aren't dating them, you are dating their parent.

* * *

> *What greater thing is there for two human*
> *souls than to find that they are joined for life.*
> —GEORGE ELIOT

849. If you want handsome strangers to stop and ask you what kind of dog you have, walk a Chinese Shar-Pei.

850. Many couples who know they will never marry continue to date because they just don't want the fun to end. These couples can be fun to associate with, but watch out for their influence!

851. Dating trivia: Only a small percentage of women ask men for a date on a regular basis.

852. Dating fact: There are over a million divorces each year in this country, and most of the newly single will remarry within two years.

853. Smiling is the best way to let someone know you are interested in them.

854. Use your home computer to keep track of all aspects of your love life.

855. Dating superstition: A young girl was told to hold a mirror over a well to see the face of her future husband.

856. Appreciate all your own good qualities. Don't shrug off all the unique qualities you have to offer a mate.

857. Trust your own judgments about dates and don't let others unduly influence your decisions. You know what is best for you!

858. Allow yourself to have plenty of fun in your life. It is great to work hard at finding a mate, but have fun while searching.

859. Here is an entire year of romantic settings to put to good use:

Spring—flower gardens, parks, meadows, pastures
Summer—beach, ocean, lakes, pools
Fall—haylofts, hayrides, nature walks, mountains
Winter—cabins, fireplaces, ski lodges

860. Keep in mind that no one is perfect and no relationship is perfect. You have to be realistic, not a dreamer!

861. Make sure your diet includes plenty of healthy foods and not just junk food. Singles are notorious for eating poorly.

862. If your love interest tells you that she wants to be "just friends," put the relationship behind you and move on.

863. If you try to kiss your date goodnight and you miss her lips, try again. Don't feel embarrassed—just laugh about it.

864. If you desperately need a date for a major social occasion, consider asking:

Someone you have a crush on
Your best friend of the opposite sex
A co-worker who is just a pal
A friend of a friend
A blind date
Your new love interest

865. The course of true love doesn't always run smoothly, so don't question your love just because things get a little bumpy.

866. Even in the very best of relationships, you won't agree on everything. Agree to disagree and just give each other some space.

867. Women complain that men are too involved in sports and that during football, basketball, and baseball seasons they forget their girlfriends are alive.

868. For a good dose of romance, reread your favorite romance novel of all time.

869. Don't be too frugal. Splurge from time to time on a fabulous night out on the town.

870. If you have a date for an evening at a dance club, wear trendy, fashionable clothes that make you stand out in a crowd.

871. Take things slowly if you and your new love interest have totally different lifestyles.

872. The hardest parts of first dates are meeting and saying good night. The more dates you go on, the easier these will get.

873. Don't just sit around waiting for a follow-up call or date. Keep busy.

874. "All's fair in love and war." Translation: Not everyone is going to play by your rules.

875. Even if you think your date is the world's best, keep your eyes wide open to get a clear picture of him.

876. Monday and Tuesday nights are great for blind dates because there isn't as much pressure as on the weekends.

877. If you are trying to be romantic, don't give a practical gift.

878. If you think your love life has problems, cheer yourself up by reading the comic strip *Cathy*.

879. Do you really want to get a date? Rent a billboard with your own personal ad on it. Be sure to have the replies go to a post office box.

880. If you are hoping to get engaged, casually mention your ring size to your lover.

881. To be a fabulous date, put yourself in your date's shoes.

882. If you want to take her on a dream date, take her on a shopping spree.

883. Women want men to call more often. Call to say:
Hello
Goodnight
You were just thinking of her
You had a great time on the date

884. If you want to stop seeing your love interest, tell him you aren't right for him. That takes the blame off of him.

885. Keep a dating diary and write down all your thoughts about every single date. Then you can go back and read what really happened, instead of relying on memories that might get distorted by your first big fight.

886. Men think is it sexy when women wear men's shirts over jeans while puttering around the house.

887. After an athletic game, tell your date that she played really well.

888. Look for a mate who can take defeat, but still hold his head above water.

889. Most people appreciate a sincere expression of affection. Don't worry about being too nice or that you will scare a date off.

890. When the occasion calls for a gift, give a homemade one to show just how important your love interest is to you.

891. Look for a mate who you have a great deal in common with, so that you can build on these interests.

892. To build a quality relationship, make sure that you both put equal importance on the relationship.

893. When you choose a mate, pick them for what they have on the inside and not just on the outside.

894. Even if you have been out of college for a long time, consider giving your steady girlfriend your fraternity pin.

895. Businesses are beginning to realize that office romances are a common part of the workplace in the nineties.

896. Dating fact: Over the past several decades, the incidence of women asking out a man has almost doubled.

Ways to Recover from a Bad First Impression:

897. Pretend it didn't happen. You will find that most people won't say anything about your silly mistakes if you don't.

898. If you make a big blunder, simply apologize in a very sincere fashion.

899. Try to explain what went wrong in a calm, upbeat manner. This isn't the time to be dramatic.

900. Be honest about the entire incident and express your embarrassment.

901. Try to turn the whole pitiful event into a funny story that the two of you can laugh about.

902. Have a friend put in a good word for you with the love interest you are trying to impress.

903. Send a note explaining that this was the first and only time in your life you acted this way.

904. When all else fails, leave and try again later.

* * *

The heart will break, but brokenly live on.
—GEORGE GORDON, LORD BYRON

905. Be nostalgic about your relationship, even if it is only months old.

906. If someone is standing closer to you than the normal conversational distance, he is probably interested in you.

907. If you are unsure about the type of clothes to wear, find a fashion mentor and copy her style until you feel secure enough to wear what you want.

908. Plan a wardrobe that fits your lifestyle. It is easy to get caught up in buying beautiful cocktail dresses, but if your dates usually take you to a ball game or other casual events, you will need informal clothes.

909. The higher your standards are for a potential mate, the smaller the number of people there will be who match your requirements. You need to balance your dreams with reality.

910. Use a lip liner to keep your lipstick from feathering. This will make your lips more kissable.

911. Never give up on your belief that your Mr./Miss right is out there for you, and don't stop looking until you find your love.

912. The more in touch you are with the kind of mate you are looking for, the more likely you will be to find that type of person.

913. Someday your search for true love will end in marriage, so make the most of your single days while you can.

914. Listen very carefully to what your heart and intuition are telling you about your current love interest.

915. You need to know when to leave your present relationship to go on to another that will better suit you. Experience is one of the best teachers to help you make this decision.

916. When dating, be smart about drinking. Follow these simple rules:
  Pace yourself
  Eat before and while you drink
  Never mix alcohol and medication
  Sip, don't gulp, your cocktail
  Beware of any date who wants you to get drunk—you are headed for trouble!

917. Dating can be expensive (entertainment, clothes, transportation, flowers, cards, etc.), so set up a dating budget to cover your costs.

918. Dating involves three kinds of risks: putting your heart on the line, learning about yourself, and forming your reputation. But remember: Without risk, there is no gain.

919. Try not to make your first date for a Saturday night. This can often make the date more stressful than it need be.

920. Women want men to show their feeling more often in relationships.

921. A recent survey of businessmen found that they like to find little love notes hidden in their briefcases. Ladies, start hiding them!

922. Tell your date that she means the world to you.

923. Look for a mate who can be counted on when you need a friend.

924. If you need to turn down a date, just say that you have to work late at the office on a big project.

925. Know the basics of romance:

Flowers	Candy
Candles	Unexpected gifts
Soft music	Cards
Poetry	Love songs

926. Before you let anyone fix you up with a blind date, find out how well they know the person.

927. Many couples who have dated for more than six months split dating expenses.

928. Stay away from singles who are involved with any type of criminal activity. You can't be together in jail—need we say more?

929. A good dating relationship gives you a wonderful sense of belonging.

930. If your love interest tells you that he isn't ready for a commitment, trust that he is telling you the truth and move on.

931. Ask a single stranger for directions to:

A trendy restaurant	A new club
A local park	Anywhere that singles hang out

932. If you want to get attention, heads will turn when you are being dragged down the street by your gigantic Great Dane.

933. Ask an attractive stranger for advice:
In a store, about what you are thinking of buying
In an airport, about the location of a certain airline
In a restaurant, about what is good to eat

934. Join a singles' group for pet lovers only. It is a great place to meet other canine lovers.

935. Some singles have a huge fear of commitment, so they stay in a relationship that they know will not lead to marriage. Unless you want to live alone, this is a fear you'll have to reckon with.

936. Buy Valentines and send them throughout the year, just to be romantic.

937. Even if you get really nervous on dates, try to avoid giggling. It makes you look childish.

938. Whisper sweet nothings into your date's ear if you want to be romantic.

939. If you feel like someone else is moving in on your date, reach over and straighten his tie, fix her collar, or make any little gesture to show that the two of you are together.

940. It is a proven fact that singles have known for centuries—everyone looks better by candlelight.

941. Get a CD player, so you can invite a date to spend the evening listening to your romantic favorites.

942. When you use an answering machine, make sure your message isn't too cute and that it doesn't mislead a prospective date into thinking you are involved with someone.

943. While waiting for love, plan your own adventure and love just might come to you while you are in:

New York City	Carmel, Calif.
Palm Beach	Chicago
London	Florence
Trinidad	The French Riviera
Kenya	Egypt

944. Dating superstition: If you want to know the depth of your lover's feelings, pick the petals off a daisy one by one while reciting "He loves me a little, he loves me a lot, he loves me madly." When you pull the last petal, you will know his true feelings.

945. If your love interest needs some time on her own, give it to her and look for a new one.

956. If you plan to use a credit card to pay for the date, carry two separate cards, so if one gets turned down, you can use the other one.

957. Some people clam up and just can't talk on first dates. Plan an activity, rather than relying solely on conversation.

958. Love takes work. Make it a priority.

959. "Love means never having to say you're sorry" is absolutely not true. Everyone makes mistakes.

What *Not* to Do after a Break-up:

960. *Don't* create the false hope of getting back together. Even though this is very easy to do, wishful thinking will only break your heart more.

961. *Don't* plead and beg with your ex to get back together. Have some pride.

962. *Don't* plan your revenge (even if it does sound sweet).

963. *Don't* blame yourself unfairly for everything that went wrong.

964. *Don't* spend too much time alone.

965. *Don't* jump right into another relationship.

966. *Don't* give up on all members of the opposite sex.

967. *Don't* let yourself become bitter or cynical.

* * *

Fortune and love befriend the bold.

—OVID

Guidelines for Couples Who Work Together:

968. Leave your work at the office. Don't discuss it on dates.

969. Have time away from each other.

970. Create a little mystery by having separate interests.

971. Spend quality time together when you concentrate on the romantic side of your relationship.

972. At the office, privately steal a kiss, pass a love note, or say sweet nothings.

973. Don't let your jobs interfere with your relationship and vice versa.

974. Keep your priorities straight—whether they are fun and games or finding a long-term romance.

975. Be discreet at all times. Never flaunt your relationship.

976. Consider keeping your relationship a secret until you know it is going to work out.

* * *

977. A disaster is a time when people need help. Reach out and help those good-looking strangers.

978. If you have extra supplies during a disaster, pass them out to other singles and mingle.

979. After a disaster, everyone has a story to tell. Listen to an attractive stranger tell his story, then tell him yours.

980. The aftermath of a major disaster is a great time to get to know other singles, as everyone's guards are down. People want to reach out to others. Take advantage of the situation.

981. If you want to meet someone famous, send her an interesting letter of introduction.

982. If you spot someone in a restaurant you would like to get to know, send a bottle of fine wine to his table with an invitation to join you.

983. Never admit to a date that you watch a lot of daytime television. You don't want her to think you are a couch potato.

984. When your date gives you a gift, thank them twice—once when you receive the gift and another time to show you really liked it.

985. You know you are becoming a couple if he calls you on the telephone whenever he feels like it.

986. It is an encouraging sign when your love interest begins to share his secrets, fears, and dreams of the future with you.

987. You have nothing to lose by going on a blind date, and you have a lot to win. Just remember the cardinal rule: Never turn a blind date down without a *great* reason.

988. If your blind date turns out to be not right for you, set her up with a friend who would be perfect for her. You never know—they could return the favor and fix you up with the love of your lifetime.

989. It is a great sign when your love interest starts saying "we" instead of "I."

990. Be the type of person who can be totally committed to a relationship.

991. If a date is going exceptionally well, find an all-night diner and continue the magic over a late-night snack.

992. Send your love interest a telegram the next time you ask her out, instead of calling her on the phone.

993. If you meet a date from a personal ad, make the first meeting short and in a well-lit public place.

994. If you are going on a blind date or with a date from a personal ad, tell a friend your plans, so that if you don't come home on time, he can start looking for you.

995. Always take your pursuit of romantic love seriously. Think of how hard you work in other areas of your life. Do the same here.

996. Strike up conversations with everyone around you. It is great practice and you might end up talking to the love of your life.

997. Make sure you understand the language of personal ads when writing them or answering them. Otherwise, you could be in for the surprise of your life.

G—Gay	A—Asian
B—Black	Bi—Bisexual
D—Divorced	D/Df—Drug and disease free
F—Female	Hisp—Hispanic
J—Jewish	M—Male
M—Married	S—Single
W—White	

998. Let your family and friends know that you want to meet quality singles.

999. Time at home in front of the television set is better spent out circulating.

1000. Do your shopping on weeknights and weekends, when you'll see more singles.

1001. Cultivate friendships with people who are out and about. They will have the best connections.

1002. Pursue finding a mate with the same gusto that you pursue your other goals and interests.

1003. It's true: Sometimes you have to kiss a lot of toads before you meet your prince.

1004. While attending adult education classes, sit in the middle of the room to have a full view of your classmates.

1005. Maintain friendships with people of all ages. You never know who knows whom.

1006. Remember that before Cinderella could meet her prince, she had to go to the ball. In other words, get out there!

1007. Before you plan your next vacation, check with your travel agent for the latest hot spots for singles.

1008. Dating trivia: Research shows that people marry those who live near them.

1009. If you think you might have a serious problem with your love life, consult your minister, priest, rabbi or family counselor.

1010. Studies prove that if you wait till you are over twenty-five to marry, you have a much better chance of staying happily married. In fact, many experts believe that no one should marry before the age of thirty.

1011. Read the singles' ads in newspapers to see if your special someone is looking for you.

1012. Never wear beige-colored clothing because you will blend into the background and this is not what you want. You want to be noticed—so wear a color that stands out.

1013. Say something to get a cute stranger's attention. Anything is better than letting your chance get away.

1014. Casually let attractive strangers know that you are available.

1015. Always stress the things you have in common with the person you want to date or are dating.

1016. Dating is a numbers game. The more people you meet, the better your odds are of getting a date. The more dates you have, the more likely you are of making it to the altar.

1017. If you spot an attractive single, strike up a conversation. If it goes well, suggest getting a cup of coffee.

1018. All of us have a natural flirt inside; you just need to learn to bring this side of you to the surface.

1019. Make a pact with your friends to pass along information about all former dates.

1020. There are several styles of flirting—the joking flirt, the friendly flirt, and the sexy flirt. Use the one that works best for you.

1021. If you are scared of dating, know that fear plus action equals self-esteem. In other words, plan a date for this weekend.

1022. Whenever you are looking for a date, adopt a self-assured demeanor.

1023. Studies show that if you date someone at work, you are four times more likely to marry them.

1024. Before you ask someone out, give her a chance to know you a little.

1025. If you feel that you are attracted to the wrong type, change your type. Don't use this as an excuse for bad relationships or for not dating.

1026. Be a hug-giver. Hugging is a great flirting technique.

1027. In a pinch, when you don't have a lot of time, hand a cute stranger your name and phone number and tell him to call you for a date.

1028. Flirting, when done properly, makes the air crackle with excitement.

1029. Being desperate is not attractive. Other singles can spot it a mile away.

1030. Before you approach an attractive stranger, try to make eye contact.

1031. If you ask someone out and he turns you down because he is involved with someone, ask him if he knows of anyone available who might be right for you.

1032. If you are looking for a date, keep in mind that dark bars are often bad places to meet people because you can have trouble making eye contact.

Easy-to-Use Lines for Grocery Store Mingling:

1033. "It looks like you love to cook."

1034. "Are we in the express line?"

1035. "It looks like you're having a party."

1036. "This dinner I'm making better be worth all this effort."

1037. "I hate standing in long lines when I am running late."

1038. "Have you ever tried this product?"

1039. "Have you been standing here a long time?"

1040. "Why don't they open up some more check-out lines?"

1041. "Can you believe that I'm standing in line for just one silly item?"

1042. "It looks like you must have a dog at home. What kind?"

1043. "If we ever get out of this line, let's go get a cup of coffee."

* * *

To love oneself is the beginning of a lifelong romance.
—OSCAR WILDE

1044. Setting up impossible expectations for your love life is a great way to end up sitting at home every Saturday night.

1045. We get our ideas of romantic love from:

Movies	Novels
Magazines	Parents
Television	Peers
Friends	Popular music

1046. Most men are looking for a mate who is sensible. After all, they are looking for a lifetime partner who will make their life easier, not more complicated.

1047. If you need to turn down a date, simply say "no" if you aren't comfortable giving a reason.

1048. Singles want to date those who share their particular sense of humor.

Looking for the Wealthy?

1049. Join a private club and search for your love among the members.

1050. Frequent exclusive resorts and keep your eyes peeled for singles.

1051. Attend excellent schools and study the students as well as the curriculum.

1052. Regularly attend charity functions that appeal to your age group.

1053. Shop, even if it is just window shopping, at elegant boutiques and get to know the salespeople. One of the clerks may just introduce you to another customer who will turn out to be the love of your life.

* * *

Easy Tips for Remembering Names:

1054. Try using a rhyme with the name:
Nancy—Fancy
Chris—Bliss
Dale—Male

1055. Break the name into syllables if it is hard to pronounce and repeat them over and over till you feel comfortable with the name.

1056. Use symbols that can help you visualize the name:
Jack—picture Little Jack Horner from the old
nursery rhyme
Debbie—imagine a Little Debbie snack cake

1057. Link the name with a person from your past. Hopefully, it won't be the name of a lover who broke your heart.

1058. Write the name down. You might want to write it a dozen times to make sure you don't forget it. It is vitally important to remember your date's name.

1059. Concentrate on the person's name when you are being introduced. This can be hard to do if you are thinking you have just met the love of your life, but do it anyway.

* * *

In its very essence, love is an appreciation, a recognition of another's value.
—ROBERT A. JOHNSON

1060. If you want to meet a celebrity, get a job with the media and use your press pass to get an introduction.

If You Are over Fifty-five and Looking for Love:

1061. Spend time at the senior citizen center and get acquainted with your peers.

1062. Go to community centers for dances that are held on weekends. This gives you a great opportunity to ask an attractive stranger for a dance.

1063. Consider moving to a retirement community, so you will be surrounded by your peers of both sexes.

1064. Ask your children to fix you up with their friends' parents.

1065. If you live in a high rise, ask the doorman if he knows of any terrific singles for you to meet. Don't be shy about asking for his help—most people love to play matchmaker.

1066. The next time you are waiting at the doctor's office, visit among the other patients.

1067. Check with your apartment manager to see if anyone living in your complex might be right for you.

1068. If you need to go to the Social Security office, look around for more than a check. Keep your eyes peeled for an available single who might change your life.

1069. As morbid as this might sound, when you attend a friend's funeral, glance around the funeral home for prospective dates. After all, you have something in common. You both knew the deceased!

1070. Check with your grandchildren about setting you up with their friends' grandparents. Children can learn at a very young age that love makes the world go round.

1071. Move in with your children. This will be a huge incentive for them to find you a spouse and home of your own.

* * *

To write a good love letter you ought to begin without knowing what you mean to say, and to finish without knowing what you have written.
—JEAN JACQUES ROUSSEAU

1072. Seal a letter with CYK (consider yourself kissed).

1073. Take things slowly in relationships where the two of you practice different religions.

1074. Before you tie the knot, come to an understanding about whether you'll have children together.

1075. Have the perfect outfit to wear to sporting events like ball games, which are a very popular date.

1076. Plan what you are going to wear for upcoming events. You don't want to be out looking for something to buy hours before a date.

1077. If you are on a limited budget, shop the stores for sales on good-quality clothing.

1078. Women want men to relax on dates and not try so hard to impress them with outrageous stories.

1079. If you need to break off a relationship, but don't want to hurt your love interest, tell her she will end up breaking your heart if you continue to see her.

1080. Want to see how Hollywood views romance? Spend Saturday afternoons viewing these movies:

To Catch a Thief	*Sleepless in Seattle*
When Harry Met Sally	*Chapter Two*
Father of the Bride	*Casablanca*
Play It Again, Sam	*Cinderella*

1081. Men love it when women dress up for a date in silk stockings and high-heeled shoes.

1082. Tell your date she should be a model. She will love you for it.

1083. Look for a mate who doesn't like to argue and who goes about life in an easy-going manner. You will be happier in the long run.

1084. When you turn down a date, state that you have plans for that particular time and can't break your commitment because your friends, boss, or family will be mad if you do.

1085. Don't misjudge a person by making assumptions about their personality based on where you met them. For example, not everyone you meet in a bookstore is a bookworm, nor is everyone in a bar is a lounge lizard.

1086. Just for fun, take a magazine quiz to determine if you are good dating material or if you are in a healthy relationship.

1087. Romantic gifts don't have to cost a fortune. Try:
Flowers from a street vendor
Love letters (100 percent free!)
Cards (very inexpensive)
Candy (small box)
Phone calls (deposit a quarter)

1088. Never think of your date as a stereotype.

1089. Have you met the man of your dreams? You can ask him to marry you on February 29th (leap year).

1090. On your date's birthday, be the first to call and wish him "Happy Birthday."

1091. Hang a banner on your front door welcoming your date when you have him over for a special evening.

1092. Learn how to cook one fabulous, romantic dinner, so you can entertain dates in your home. (Yes, men should learn to cook, too.)

1093. While you are looking for love, eliminate needless worries from your life. You don't need any added stress.

1094. Men like women who are healthy-looking, not waif-thin.

1095. If you want to meet someone you have a crush on, hang out where he goes and wangle an introduction from one of his friends.

1096. Never tell a prospective date that you are in a dating dry spell. You want her to think you are desirable.

1097. If a date gives you a present, when you thank her, mention how the two of you can use the gift. You want her to think of a future together.

1098. Mail your date a safety pin with a note saying you are stuck on him.

1099. Ask the attractive single at church if you can borrow his Bible or read over his notes from the morning service.

Phases of True Love:
1. The search for that special someone
2. Meeting someone you feel attracted to and want to date
3. Sensing a hint of romance between the two of you
4. The development of feelings and good impressions, and the making of memories
5. Building true intimacy and continuing the relationship

1100. If you see someone you'd die for, pretend you're sick and ask for their help.

1101. Call your favorite radio DJ and request a special song and dedication.

1102. Take an interest in the work of that mysterious someone, to get a sense of where they're coming from and where they're going.

Romantic Calls at Work: Info Your Secretary Needs to Get When You Can't Take a Call Yourself

1103. What was the name of the caller?

1104. Will the caller call back? If so, when?

1105. Should you call back?

1106. Did your secretary have any impressions from the phone call?

1107. Your secretary should try to get both a work and a home telephone number..

1108. What is the correct spelling and pronunciation of the caller's name?

1109. What time did the call come into your office?

1110. Did the caller give a reason for the call?

* * *

1111. The top ten careers that impress dates the most are:

Doctor	Lawyer
CEO	Diplomat
Pilot	Investment banker
Author	Government official
Conductor	Filmmaker

1112. If you meet a date through the personal ads, meet in an area of the city you know well and can get to easily.

1113. Don't give your home address to a date until you feel absolutely certain that it will be safe to do so. That may take a couple of dates.

1114. High school reunions are one of the all-time best settings for a date. Plan to take someone special. Or, if you are brave enough to face your classmates without a date, go alone to search for love.

1115. Before you go out looking to meet someone to date, get your best friend to give you a pep talk.

1116. When you are looking for love, wear your favorite clothes, so you will feel comfortable and look good.

1117. Read a romantic novel to remind yourself what you are missing if you don't get out there and find your true love.

1118. Before you go out, listen to a motivational tape to get you in the right frame of mind.

1119. True love stories don't have endings.

1120. As a general rule, "nice" guys make better lifetime partners than "macho" types.

1121. Make a Sunday afternoon seem like a holiday by planning a special date.

1122. When you receive a promotion at work, make a date to go out and celebrate.

1123. It is great to put your best foot forward when you are on a date, but be careful not to sound like you are tooting your own horn.

1124. When a date takes you out for dinner, don't overeat.

1125. If your date is serious about finding a spouse, he may look carefully at your spending habits, so be careful about overspending. He won't want a spouse who could hurt his financial future.

1126. Many people believe that companionship is the number one reason to get married. Life is more fun when you have someone to share it with.

1127. Infatuation can make you oblivious to your love interest's feelings.

1128. Love gives you the courage and strength to go out into the world feeling stronger and happier.

1129. If you are looking for love, consult the following to get ideas for meeting singles:
Yellow pages
Local city magazine
Public library

1130. Take plenty of photographs on your dates to use later as gifts for your love interest.

1131. When your date gets sick:
Offer to take her to a doctor
Call her mom
Send flowers
Bring interesting magazines
Visit to help her pass the time
Send get-well cards

1132. There are trade-offs in all relationships. You are going to have to compromise in order to make true love run smoothly.

1133. Many singles fear they will lose their sense of autonomy if they become deeply involved with another person. This fear is especially common among older singles.

1134. Many times one partner is ready for marriage, while the other isn't. Before you let the world's best partner slip away, think carefully about letting her go.

1135. When you stand, hold your shoulders back, but don't look like you are in the armed forces. You want to appear confident, not like a Marine sergeant.

1136. Take an interest in the world around you and let it shine in your eyes. You want people to think you are an informed, curious person with an exciting life.

1137. Work at projecting a relaxed, open manner with your body language.

1138. Get involved in a loving relationship so you can give and receive love.

1139. Find a mate so you will have someone to grow old with.

1140. Improve your sense of self-esteem, so you will be better able to handle the ups and downs of a long-term relationship without taking things so personally.

Easy Weight Loss Tips to Get You into Shape Before Your Next Big Date:

1141. When you fix a meal, measure the portions and serve small amounts.

1142. Save part of your meal at restaurants and bring it home in a doggie bag to use for another small meal.

1143. When you have free time, spend it exercising.

1144. Dwell on the positive sides of your dieting efforts, not on the few pounds that sneak back on you.

1145. Use butter-flavored sprinkles instead of butter when you cook.

1146. Force yourself to walk to your destinations when feasible.

1147. Go to the gym before you fix dinner—it will help curb your appetite.

1148. Don't keep high-calorie junk food in your house. It is just too hard to resist.

1149. Eliminate cheese from your sandwiches. It is easy to do and makes a big difference in the number of calories in your lunch.

1150. Take up jogging or power walking with your love interest.

1151. Stock your cabinets with low-calorie foods.

1152. Chew low-calorie gum instead of eating a chocolate bar.

1153. Buy yourself a gift when you reach your desired goal weight.

* * *

1154. If you see a cute stranger, ask his help (which you might really need) in walking your 180-pound mastiff.

1155. If you think you can't control a mastiff, walk a bull mastiff. (You will still look like you need help walking this dog, as they are powerful pooches!)

1156. Walk two or more dogs to get a cute stranger's attention. Our two golden retrievers and little cocker spaniel think this is one of the best ways to meet people.

1157. When you are going to pick up your date, listen to classical music instead of hard rock.

1158. Some people will continue to date someone while waiting for someone better to come along. Check your love interest's motives if you think they are just marking time with you.

1159. An easy way to let a stranger know you are interested is to gaze at him from time to time. Please note that we didn't say stare him down!

1160. Never chew gum on a date. It looks tacky!

1161. You might want to consider buying a fax machine to send cute messages to your new love interest. However, don't send messages to an office fax—the boss might get them instead!

1162. Be sensitive—never embarrass a date.

1163. Caress your significant other.

1164. If you are at a party and see a good-looking stranger, tell him that the host suggested you should come over and meet him.

1165. In the old days, young girls were told to sleep with a mirror under their pillows, so they would see the face of their future mate in their dreams.

1166. If you see a cute stranger, just say, "I have to know, are you married?" This will get things off to an interesting start.

1167. Postcards are believed to cast a shadow over budding romances, so many lovers only send letters.

1168. If your love interest tells you she needs to spend more time with her friends, you are probably headed for a break-up.

1169. Both men and women are looking for someone who is a friend as well as a romantic partner.

1170. When you compliment a date, do it in front of others. Your date will appreciate the added attention.

1171. If you are out on a date and run out of money and your date isn't carrying any cash, don't panic. Call a friend.

1172. If you become ill on a date and have to cut it short, send flowers to her the next day.

1173. There can be many great loves in a lifetime. So don't panic if your significant other dumps you.

1174. Still need a little romance? Watch your favorite romantic movie again.

1175. The opposite of true love is not hate, but indifference. If you are feeling indifferent, reconsider your romance.

1176. Never put your love interest up on a pedestal. It gets lonely up there.

1177. If you feel you are seriously starting to fall for that special someone, browse a jewelry store for diamond engagement rings.

1178. Women don't like men who put their buddies before their girlfriends. Get your priorities straight.

1179. If you are hitting the bars to look for a date, wear work attire for happy hours and casual clothes at other times.

1180. If you are dating someone of a different race, tread lightly, as this may make your relationship more complicated.

1181. Maintain your clothes with fine care and quality dry cleaning. (This also means that you shouldn't use your floor as a closet.)

1182. Splurge on a drop-dead, "can't keep the dates away" outfit for those special times out on the town.

1183. If you want to end a relationship, tell her that you will end up breaking her heart because you aren't ready for a serious involvement. This will put the blame on you, not her.

1184. Women like men who let them plan some dates.

1185. States with the highest number of marriages:

California	Florida
Illinois	Massachusetts
Michigan	Nevada
New York	Ohio
Pennsylvania	Tennessee

1186. Men are looking for a mate who will take care of them when they are sick.

1187. ABCs of positive dating:

A—adventurous	N—neat
B—bright	O—observant
C—charming	P—pleasant
D—dazzling	Q—quality
E—enjoyable	R—romantic
F—funny	S—sexy
G—good-natured	T—tasteful
H—honest	U—upbeat
I—inquisitive	V—virtuous
J—judicious	W—warm
K—kind	X—exemplary
L—lively	Y—young at heart
M—mature	Z—zany

1188. Send your love interest a love letter by special messenger.

1189. On a dating anniversary, give a gift that would have special significance to your date.

1190. On your date's birthday, bake a cake from scratch. It is often the little, thoughtful gestures that make a huge difference in the quality of a relationship.

1191. Stick to your normal routine on the day of an important date, so you won't get as nervous.

1192. An old wives' tale suggests that, to attract a dream lover, you should stick two pins into a candle and light it. When the flame burns down to the pins, the lover will appear. (It seems to us you would want to buy a very short candle!)

1193. If you are going to tell someone that you love them for the first time, tell them while riding in a horse-drawn carriage.

Key Tips for Writing a Personal Ad For Men:

1194. Use words that make you sound mature.

1195. Make sure to emphasize your height if you are tall.

1196. Express your interest in diverse activities and hobbies—a well-rounded person is an attractive person.

1197. State that you are a professional (if you are) and employed (if you are).

For Women:

1198. Use the word "pretty" when describing yourself.

1199. Mention favorite activities that express your personality. If you are a city girl and like sophisticated pursuits, list a few. If you are physically active, mention a few of your favorite sports.

1200. Let the readers of your ad know the kind of man you are looking for. If you would prefer to meet a well-educated men, make this clear. If you would prefer to meet a man who shares your religion, mention this. This way, you won't waste anybody else's time.

* * *

Persons are to be loved; things are to be used.
—REUEL HOWE

1201. If you want to meet a celebrity, try to get an invitation to a party he will be attending.

1202. If you want to meet a specific person, become friends with her friends. The world is a lot smaller than you might think.

1203. If you have a crush on someone, find out from her secretary where she is having lunch, stop by her table, and introduce yourself. Keep it short—you want to make it seem like an accidental meeting.

1204. If you live at home with your parents and you are over twenty-one, keep this information under wraps in the early stages of your relationship.

1205. You don't need to tell a prospective date about your good qualities or that your friends think you are a good catch. Let her figure these things out for herself.

1206. It is a proven fact: If you put more romantic gestures into your relationship, the relationship will improve.

1207. Blind dates are great because they provide you with an opportunity to improve your dating skills.

1208. If your dates are becoming more casual, more spur-of-the-moment, it means one of two things: The relationship is getting serious or he is taking you for granted.

1209. Want to know where you stand with your current flame? Check to see if you are number one on her speed dial.

1210. Stay young at heart if you want to be considered a great potential mate.

1211. When you meet your significant other's mom, bring her flowers.

1212. The first time you say "I love you," have your favorite music playing in the background.

1213. Once you become a dating couple, create little rituals like:
Kissing hello
Kissing good-bye
Calling every night at 11:00 P.M. to say goodnight
Having a standing Saturday night date
Holding hands when you say grace
Having a mid-week standing date

1214. Refrain from male-bashing while on a date.

1215. Apathy is the number one relationship destroyer.

1216. Be careful of giving mixed signals to your dates.

1217. If your love interest's parents know all about you, that is a really great sign that your relationship is moving in the right direction.

1218. If your friend sets you up on a date, but it doesn't work out, thank him anyway and have him keep you in mind for other fix-ups.

1219. When you first meet with a date from the personal ads, arrange to meet during the day.

1220. If you decide to place a personal ad, you don't have to tell anybody about it unless you want to. It can be your little secret.

1221. To beat an attack of the stomach butterflies before a date, drink a glass of seltzer or ginger ale with a dash of Angostura bitters.

1222. Believe it or not, researchers claim the scent that turns men on the most is cinnamon.

1223. To be an enjoyable date, let go of your need to always be right.

1224. Take each phase of the dating process one step at a time. In other words, don't plan your wedding before the end of your first date!

1225. Guard your reputation carefully. Don't do anything that might make others regard you in a bad light.

1226. Don't use the old excuse of hanging on to a past relationship to keep you from getting out into the dating scene.

1227. You don't have to be ready for marriage just because you are dating.

1228. It is always a good thing to have a dating emergency kit on hand that includes:

Needle and thread	Spot remover
Clothing brush	Spare hosiery

1229. Women are looking for a man who is a good listener and who will provide a strong shoulder to cry on if the need arises.

1230. Men want a woman whom they find attractive and whom they will be proud to be seen with.

1231. Most men want a woman who will make a wonderful mother for their children.

1232. Look for a mate who will take your side in an argument between you and her friends.

1233. Are you really serious about finding a mate? Post a reward of at least $500 to the person who introduces you to the person you marry. We guarantee this will get your friends busy setting you up on dates!

1234. If you get a cold sore on the day of a date, put a little concealer over it to make it less noticeable.

1235. Drop your love interest if he is using you. You want someone who wants you for yourself, not for what you can do for him.

1236. If your love interest doesn't respond to your overtures, she probably isn't interested in you.

1237. Men soften their voices when they talk to women they are interested in. How does his voice sound when he talks to you?

1238. If you want to be creative, say "I love you" in another language:

French—*Je t'aime*　　　German—*Ich liebe dich*
Italian—*Te amo*　　　Japanese—*Ai shite masu*
Spanish—*Te quiero*

1239. Even if you are extremely nervous, never giggle after a kiss goodnight.

1240. No peeking—always keep your eyes closed during a goodnight kiss.

1241. When making an introduction, introduce the younger person to the older person. It might help you to remember the adage, "Age before beauty."

1242. If you use a professional matchmaker, make sure she/he is discreet.

1243. Make sure the pitch of your voice is not too high or your voice will be irritating to your dates. Work with a voice coach if you need to.

1244. When you tell a joke, have it memorized and tell it in a conversational manner.

1245. If you aren't good at telling jokes, don't tell one.

1246. A man should always walk next to the curb on busy streets while his date walks on the inside. Your date will think you are quite gallant.

1247. Before a big date, take a nice, long shower. You might even try singing a romantic tune to get you in the mood for love.

1248. If you are really nervous about picking up your date, talk to your best buddy on a car phone all the way to her house.

1249. To relieve tension on a date, go into a restroom and do a few stretching exercises.

1250. No matter what happens on your date, try to keep your sense of humor.

1251. If you are really nervous about a date, talk to your date before you go. Tell him how you feel. He is probably feeling the same way.

1252. Try to remain open and flexible about the outcome of all your dates.

1253. Remember that dating is a fun, positive adventure, and a bad date is not the end of the world.

1254. After a break-up, put your friendship with your ex on hold until you have both moved on and are comfortably involved in other romantic relationships.

1255. The very next date you go on could be the dream date of a lifetime. Isn't that an exciting thought?

1256. To put yourself in a good mood before a date, think of all the fun times you have had on dates in the past.

1257. Homecoming weekends are a great time to look for a date. Check out your old flames and all your favorite classmates.

1258. It is easier to look for love in the summertime because more singles are out and about. Put your summer vacation to good use looking for Miss/Mr. Right.

1259. If you are a big gambler, get some help before dating. No one wants to find that you pawned the engagement ring to pay off your gambling debts.

1260. The number two reason that singles give for wanting to get married is to have children.

1261. Singles take note—infatuation will lead you to make hasty decisions.

1262. Love is patient and trusting, and it makes you feel good about everything.

1263. Many single parents fear they will be unable to find a partner who will make a good step-parent for their children. This isn't necessarily true. There are millions of wonderful singles out there to choose from.

1264. Being a part of a couple is one of the most wonderful feelings in the world.

1265. If you want to impress your date in a big way, take her to the circus and have the ringmaster express your love for her.

1266. Use fall scenery to inspire romance:
Rake leaves together and bury one another in them
Hold hands during a tour of a haunted house
Snuggle on a hayride
Pack a gourmet picnic and enjoy the gorgeous fall leaves
Keep warm by cuddling at a nighttime football game

1267. You know your love interest is crazy about you if he lets you borrow his favorite stuff.

1268. Drop your love interest if he thinks only of himself and his needs.

1269. Fashion 101: Striped tops and plaid bottoms rarely make a fashion statement.

1270. Always use a beautiful stamp to mail a love letter.

1271. Be the first person to end a phone call. You want to come across as confident, not needy.

1272. Be cool, even if you haven't had a date in years. Act like you date all the time.

1273. Until you are involved in a serious relationship, date more than one person at a time. This will help you stay relaxed about your love life.

1274. Do you want to put fabulous ideas into your significant other's head? Take him on a stroll through Tiffany's and casually stop in front of the engagement rings.

1275. Try to keep your first three dates short. Each of these can be a little longer than the last, but still be brief. Remember: Keep them short and sweet.

1276. Watch your friends if you think they might try to steal your boyfriend or girlfriend.

1277. Age is a lot like love—it can't be hidden. Don't even try!

1278. Don't reveal too much about yourself on early dates. If things work out you'll have plenty of time to tell your secrets. If things don't work out, you'll be glad that you didn't reveal too much.

1279. To relieve tension on a date, try a physical activity such as hiking, whitewater rafting, or bicycling.

How to Deal with Shyness:

1280. Everyone suffers from shyness during their dating days at one time or another. It doesn't mean that you are a dating failure.

1281. Concentrate on making your date feel comfortable.

1282. Only date people who are nice and who make you feel good about yourself.

1283. Focus on developing a new, more positive self-image.

1284. View shyness as a trait that holds you back in social situations, not as a cute trait that endears you to members of the opposite sex.

1285. Force yourself to act as if you are confident. Nobody will know the difference.

* * *

Not to alter one's faults is to be faulty indeed.
—CONFUCIUS

1286. If you want to learn more about how the opposite sex thinks, read the current issues of popular male- or female-oriented magazines.

1287. Always keep your word. If you tell someone that you love them, you'd better be telling the truth!

1288. Once you find someone special to date, make time for him even if you have a hectic schedule.

1289. Place your significant other equal to your career if you think this is the person you want to marry.

1290. Keep your ring finger unadorned, so that it won't look like you are wearing an engagement or wedding band.

1291. If you are tender-hearted, don't mistake sympathy for love.

1292. Be a great date even if your date is an idiot. This can be a test of your self-control.

1293. As you get older, don't lower your standards just because you haven't found the love of your life. Just make sure your standards are realistic.

How to Look Great in a Computer Dating Service Video:

1294. Even if you have the world's best-looking white shirt, don't wear it. You will end up looking washed out on your video.

1295. Have the tape made when you can spend plenty of time getting yourself ready for the video. Don't make your appointment at the end of a busy work day. You want to look fresh, not dead tired.

1296. You will probably be nervous, so take along a friend.

1297. Plan in advance what you are going to say.

1298. Dress up! Look nice! You don't have to wear a suit, but we recommend it.

1299. Talk to the people at the dating service for advice about your video.

1300. Relax. If it turns out to be the world's worst film, you can tape it again.

1301. Practice what you are going to say. Try to sound conversational, not rehearsed.

* * *

1302. Do you need inspiration from young lovers? These ladies all became brides before the age of sixteen:
Eleanor of Aquitaine   Mary Queen of Scots
Marie Antoinette

1303. It is a sign that your relationship is moving forward when your love interest calls you for no other reason than to hear your voice.

1304. If your love interest is affectionate with you in front of her friends, this means that they are aware that you are an important part of her life.

1305. To make a first date easier, try to get to know as much as you can about the person before you go out. Talk on the telephone a few times beforehand.

1306. Meeting through the personal ads is becoming more and more popular. Some singles have had great success this way.

1307. If you want a good bottle of wine for your next romantic picnic, but your cash flow is limited, try a bottle of domestic chardonnay.

1308. If you are someone who doesn't smile a great deal, practice smiling at strangers. It will make you more approachable.

1309. If you are experiencing a sudden lack of self-esteem, don't let it stop you from meeting other people or from going out on a date.

1310. Even if you have had a string of bad dates recently, it doesn't mean that your next date will turn out that way.

1311. Many singles who are afraid to get out and look for love rationalize that they don't have enough time in their busy lives for the dating scene. Make finding a mate a top goal in your life.

1312. Valentine's Day Trivia:
This holiday has been observed since the Middle Ages
Cards were originally intended to be mailed anonymously
Red roses are currently the most popular flowers sold
The United States, England, France, and Canada
are the countries where the holiday is most popular

1313. If your love interest listens to your problems and shows a sincere interest in them, then you know he is more than just a date. He is, more importantly, your friend.

1314. Pass along secondhand compliments to your dates. They will love you for it.

1315. If your date has a great sense of humor, tell him so.

1316. If you want to turn down a date, say you are flattered by the invitation but not interested in dating at this time in your life. You might say that your schedule just doesn't give you any free time for socializing.

1317. Look for a mate who is humble, even when he has a lot to boast about. He will be easier to live with than his bragging buddies.

How to Ask Others for a Set-Up:

1318. Set up a specific time to talk to your friend/acquaintance that is convenient and suits his busy schedule.

1319. Ask for matchmaking help only from people you respect and who are good judges of character.

1320. When you meet to talk about a set-up, make your time together fun and upbeat. You want this person to do you a favor.

1321. When you ask for help in getting introduced to available singles, be quick about it. Nobody wants to hear the entire story of your love life.

1322. Give a good description of the type of person you want to date, so that your matchmaking friend won't have to guess.

1323. Listen closely to what your friend has to say. Is he truly interested in setting you up?

1324. Even if he can't matchmake for you now, ask him to keep thinking of possible singles for you. Thank him for meeting with you.

1325. If he does set you up on a date, let him know how the first date went and if you have plans to go out again.

1326. If he set you up, but the date didn't go well, don't criticize his choice.

* * *

1327. If you know what your love interest's dream date would be, plan that activity for the coming weekend to give her a date she won't soon forget.

1328. If you have been dating someone for awhile and are starting to repeat the same old activities, exchange lists of ten new things you would like to do.

1329. Carry your significant other's picture in your wallet.

1330. Are you looking for a date that is out of this world? Attend a meeting of the Mutual UFO Network (MUFON) and mingle with any single member.

1331. If you are looking for a sports fan, shop at sports memorabilia stores.

1332. Unless you are dating a psychic, don't expect your significant other to have ESP. Tell your date what you like. Ask for what you need.

1333. Do you want to know what love is all about? Read 1 Corinthians in the Bible.

1334. Think of meeting a date from the personal ads as a great romantic adventure.

1335. Look for a mate who keeps your confidences.

1336. Keep these items on hand in case you bring a date back to your place:
> Great music of two types, such as classical and rock
> A variety of beverages
> Snack foods
> Ingredients for an easy-to-make dinner
> Fresh flowers
> Candles

1337. When you are planning your dating wardrobe, don't forget that shoes are an important part. Fine leather shoes complete a nice outfit.

1338. Back off when your love interest tells you he needs to date other people.

1339. Women wish their boyfriends would take them out dancing for an entire evening at a romantic nightclub.

1340. If you want to break things off without causing too much pain to your love interest, just say that you don't fit in with his friends, family, or lifestyle. This takes him off of the hot seat.

1341. Dating trivia: The number of single men over fifteen in the United States:
Never married—28,804,618
Widowed— 2,377,589
Divorced— 6,957,466

1342. The number of single women over fifteen in the United States:
Never married—23,755,235
Widowed—12,121,939
Divorced—9,626,577

Before Beginning a Conversation with an Attractive Stranger:

1343. Pick someone who looks friendly and receptive.

1344. Wait for an appropriate time to make your approach.

1345. Never interrupt the attractive stranger's conversation with another person if you can help it.

1346. Select a great opening remark that will make a good first impression.

1347. Keep your greeting simple, so you don't overwhelm them.

1348. Be sincere, yet fun.

1349. Give yourself a big pat on the back for approaching them, no matter how it turns out.

* * *

A good woman inspires a man,
A brilliant woman interests him,
A beautiful woman fascinates him,
A sympathetic woman gets him.
—HELEN ROWLAND

1350. Studies reveal that men like women to ask them out the first time, instead of waiting for them to make the first move.

1351. Turn to your date and tell her she is different from anyone you have ever dated. This will do wonders for your relationship.

1352. If your date is wearing a wonderful-smelling cologne, tell her so.

1353. After meeting a special person, tell her that you are glad the two of you have crossed paths.

1354. If you place an ad in the personals, you can screen your replies. If you don't like any of them, no one will make you meet them. What do you have to lose?

1355. Look for a mate who will admit her mistakes to you. This means she trusts you and doesn't feel the need to put up a false front.

1356. Before going on a big date, have your makeup applied by a makeup artist. Watch the artist closely, so you can do it yourself the next time.

1357. If it isn't love, it just might be:
Friendship	Lust
Infatuation	A crush

1358. If you *like* your significant other as well as love her, you are on your way to having a fabulous romance.

1359. Dump your love interest if she is sneaky and you feel insecure in the relationship.

1360. When you kiss a date goodnight, leave him wanting more.

1361. When you are making introductions, pronounce people's names clearly so that the people you are introducing don't have to ask twice.

1362. Join a coed softball league. It will help keep you fit, and you might meet that special someone.

1363. If you like to read, browse your favorite bookstore and ask an attractive stranger his opinion on a popular new novel. If he hasn't read it, ask him to recommend something.

1364. Even though you might be nervous, keep your voice at a comfortable volume. Many people tend to get loud when they are nervous.

1365. Remember the cardinal rule of joke telling: Never, ever tell a racist joke.

1366. Men should always let a date walk through doorways first. This shows respect for her.

1367. Want to impress your date? Pick her up in a limousine!

1368. For guys only: Shave before you go out on a date.

1369. Never put off your search for true love. You don't want Mr./Miss Right to marry someone else.

1370. When you buy an engagement ring, buy the best one you can afford. After all, she may wear it her entire life.

1371. Ladies: Keep your makeup subtle but flattering.

1372. If you want a relationship to work out, start thinking of it as a long-term one.

1373. Mail your significant other a pretty antique key to represent the key to your heart.

1374. Start planning your Valentine's Day celebrations in January to make sure it is one fabulous day.

1375. Are you looking for a brilliant mate? Check with Mensa, an organization whose members all have high IQs.

1376. Look closely at your dating history. Do you have an area where certain problems keep popping up? If you do, plan to work on it

1377. Be extra careful if you choose to date a daddy's girl or a mama's boy.

1378. Just before you open the door to your date, take several slow, deep breaths.

1379. Before you go out looking for love, get a relaxing massage from a professional masseur.

1380. Everyone is looking for a date whom they can be proud of, so stop using four-letter words.

1381. Many singles want to get married to gain social acceptance. The world often regards you as more stable and grown-up if you are married.

1382. If you want to heat things up between the two of you, serve:

Herbal tea	Hot, spiced cider
Hot buttered rum	Cocoa made from scratch with marshmallows

1383. If your love interest says he needs space, he is telling you that he either wants to date other people or doesn't want to be serious at this time.

1384. Experiment with different activities on dates to find out what you both enjoy the most.

1385. Stay away from singles who can't look you straight in the eye.

What to Do after a Bad Break-Up:

1386. Get back all the stuff she borrowed from you.

1387. Be sure she gives you back the keys to your car—you don't want her to drive it into a river.

1388. Take back her set of house keys. You might want to change your locks if it was a really ugly break-up.

1389. Inform all your friends that you are no longer dating her.

1390. Put the word out that you are back in circulation (when you are ready to start dating again).

1391. Take her picture out of your wallet. You don't want a new love interest to spot it in there months from now.

1392. Erase her name from your little black book.

1393. Take down her picture at your house and on your desk at the office.

1394. Consider getting rid of all the cards and letters she sent you.

1395. Tell your friends what happened before they hear her version of the break-up.

1396. Mourn the loss of the relationship. This will take time.

1397. Once you decide that the relationship is history, totally let go of her emotionally.

1398. Get comfortable being on your own again. It will take some adjustment but it will happen.

1399. Write your feelings down in a journal.

* * *

Charm is the ability to make someone else think that both of you are wonderful.
—EDGAR MAGNIM

1400. Formulate a master plan for your love life. If you know what you want, you are halfway to getting it.

1401. Want to become a member of your significant other's family? Men—get to be the best of buddies with her dad. Women—try becoming one of his mom's closest friends.

1402. If your date is late or your friend spots your love interest talking to an attractive stranger, don't jump to conclusions. Be cool and wait for an explanation.

1403. A quality relationship will help meet your emotional needs. However, you need to meet most of your emotional needs yourself.

1404. When you are involved in a relationship, remember to celebrate these occasion together:

Birthdays	Valentine's Day
Dating anniversaries	Thanksgiving
Christmas/Hanukkah	New Year's Eve

General Rules for When to Begin Dating:

1405. For the first time: Depends on parental permission, emotional maturity, peer pressure, and local customs.

1406. After break-ups: When you feel ready or when you are no longer on the rebound.

1407. After a divorce: At least six months to a year.

1408. After a spouse's death: At least one year, and then only when you feel ready.

* * *

In Conversations, Refrain From:

1409. Using archaic phrases that make you sound out of touch. For example, don't call a woman a girl, or use the words "groovy" or "keen" as compliments (except ironically).

1410. Making slang a big part of your vocabulary if you are over twenty-one.

1411. Spreading gossip of any kind. You want your friends to think you are a good-hearted soul, not a nasty bearer of bad news.

1412. Talking a subject to death. This makes you seem as if you have limited areas of interest.

* * *

1413. If you have a job that involves technical areas of expertise, don't bore your dates with the details.

1414. On your date's birthday, sing "Happy Birthday" to her (even if you sing off-key).

1415. The best gifts to give him:
  CDs
  Tools
  Books
  A hammock
  Tickets to an upcoming event
  A gift certificate to a new restaurant
  Lawn service for a year
  Magazine subscriptions
  A framed photograph of the two of you

1416. One dating superstition held that love letters had to be written in ink, or the lover's feelings would fade.

1417. At the next party you attend, walk up to an attractive stranger and tell her she is the best-looking person at the party.

1418. If your date gives you a special gift for no particular occasion, you are on your way to becoming a couple. Sit back and enjoy the journey.

1419. When your date gives you a gift that you don't particularly like, wear it at least once, so you won't hurt his feelings.

1420. If you take out a personal ad, hire a professional matchmaker, or join a dating service, pat yourself on the back for taking action in your love-life department.

1421. Drop by your love interest's house tonight with flowers and a nice bottle of wine.

1422. Look for a mate who will help you with your work or a project that is important to you. You want a lifetime helpmate. If he won't help you when you are dating, he definitely won't help you after you get married.

1423. If your love interest never asks about your life, but talks constantly about his own, consider finding someone new.

1424. Lose your gum before you try to kiss your date.

1425. When you first meet someone, pronounce your name clearly and extend your hand.

1426. If your love interest has pets, behave affectionately toward them if possible. Pet the cat or talk to the parrot. (This doesn't work with fish, though!)

1427. If you want expert advice about your love life, try writing to an advice columnist.

1428. To help develop your sense of humor, attend comedy clubs and read books by comedians.

1429. After a date, soak in a hot tub and analyze how the evening went.

1430. Beware: Some single people don't want to have children (or more children), and they don't date anyone seriously, fearing their love interest will want a family eventually.

1431. If your love interest claims he isn't good at long-term relationships, find someone who is.

1432. Never date anyone you find intimidating after several dates. A good relationship should make you feel comfortable, not uptight.

1433. If you want to get noticed, wear a striking black and white outfit to walk your dalmatian puppy.

1434. Or if you like firemen, walk your dalmatian in front of a firehouse.

1435. Some single people will stay in a relationship that doesn't have a future simply because they need a date for upcoming events.

1436. Don't stay in a relationship when in your heart you know that it's a lost cause.

1437. Sing along with love songs on the radio.

1438. Read a passage of your favorite love poem to your significant other.

1439. Buy your love interest a copy of your favorite novel and write a romantic inscription inside.

1440. In a quality relationship, you will feel a sense of responsibility for your significant other.

1441. Memorize a song to serenade your date. If possible, do it under her window with a guitar accompaniment.

1442. In winter months, keep fit by joining a group of walkers at your local shopping mall. You never know whom you might meet there!

1443. Dating superstition: A woman was supposed to be on the lookout for meeting two men in a row on New Year's Day because, if she met them, she would have a serious love affair by the end of the next year.

1444. Stand back if you love interest says he isn't sure what he wants from your relationship.

1445. Learn to change a flat tire in case you get one while on a date.

1446. Be casual if you run into your ex while you are out on a date with a new love interest. You don't want to spoil your evening with a messy scene.

1447. If you look up and spot your parents sitting at a nearby table while you are on a date, be sure to acknowledge them and consider inviting them to join you.

1448. Listen to what your current love interest's exes have to say about him. Some of what you hear may be due to sour grapes, but remember: Where there is smoke, there is usually fire.

1449. Women are turned off by men who need too much attention from the women in their lives. They don't want to have to "mother" their dates.

1450. If you don't like the way your loved one dresses, buy him something snazzy for your next date. Better yet, ask him if he would like to go shopping together.

1451. Attend a gallery opening for a hot new artist.

1452. Men want their girlfriends to keep the intimate details of their relationship private and not discuss them with their friends.

1453. If your date is waiting for you to get ready to go out, make it snappy.

Creative Tips for Using a Name Tag to Help You Meet Someone Special:

1454. Instead of writing your name, write the name of some famous person you admire.

1455. Write your name in an unusual manner, so people will notice it.

1456. Use a symbol or funny phrase after your name to start up a conversation.

1457. Write illegibly. This way people *have* to ask your name.

1458. Wear your name tag sideways, so it will take a stranger longer to read it. This gives you time to start a conversation.

1459. Forget your name tag when everyone is supposed to wear one. You will stand out in the crowd. Plus, anyone who wants to talk to you will have to ask your name.

1460. Wear your tag on your sleeve or belt to get attention.

1461. Decorate your name tag; you don't have to paint a masterpiece but be creative.

* * *

Lost time is never found again.
—BENJAMIN FRANKLIN

1462. If you have a pet, take it to the vet for an annual checkup. While there, make friends with an attractive stranger in the waiting room. After all, you have a love of animals to build on.

1463. Before you tease a date, make sure he has a healthy sense of humor.

1464. After a great first date, send a note thanking your escort for the evening.

1465. If you want someone to know you are interested, wink.

1466. Be silly—send him a big bag of gummy bears with a note asking him to be your teddy bear.

1467. Throw a surprise party for your love interest when one of these events occurs:
A promotion at work   A major goal is reached
A move to a new place   A big birthday

1468. After a fabulous date, tell your escort that it was one of the best dates you have ever been on.

1469. Men like it when women lean their heads on their shoulder during a movie.

1470. Laugh *with*, not *at* your date.

1471. Give *him* a box of chocolates or send *him* some flowers for a change.

1472. If your apartment or house looks tired or old-fashioned, try a little redecoration. You don't need to spend a lot of money—fresh paint can lift a room all on its own, and it's inexpensive. Better yet, throw a painting party and ask your friends to bring their friends.

1473. Spray your cologne on all the cards that you send him to make them more romantic.

1474. If you want to entertain in style, you will need:

Dinner plates	Salad plates
Coffee mugs	Serving bowls
Dessert sets	Platters
Goblets	Candlesticks
Silverware	Ice bucket
Wineglasses	Coasters

1475. Start giving out more hugs.

1476. Someone once said, "Love at first sight is often cured by a second glance."

1477. If you wear eyeglasses, always remove them before a long kiss.

1478. One of the advantages of using the personal ads is that you can tell a lot about a person by reading a note from them. Do they have nice handwriting? Do they use correct grammar and spelling?

1479. When you place an ad in the classifieds, be specific about the type of person you want to meet. Ask yourself: Am I being realistic? Is the ad fun to read?

1480. If your significant other refuses to make a commitment after a reasonable period of time, and if you want to get married, move on.

1481. If your love interest is inconsiderate to your family or friends, break it off.

1482. To relax before an important date, try a bathing ritual that includes:
Playing music in the background
Burning candles around your tub
Sipping a warm beverage in the winter, a cool one
in the summer
Bathing with scented soap
Drying yourself with plush, colorful towels
Using bath gels, beads, or bubble bath

1483. Men like women who will let their hair down and go barefoot on a picnic in the summertime.

1484. Go up to a pretty stranger at a party and tell her that people are always telling you how nice she is.

1485. If you want to stop seeing your love interest, but don't want to break his heart, tell him that you just don't deserve him.

1486. A woman wants a man who will show a genuine interest in her life.

1487. Women love surprises. Send flowers to her office for no particular occasion, just to show her you are thinking about her.

1488. Buy him a nice cologne and ask him to try it. (Avoid the one your ex-boyfriend used!)

1489. Proceed cautiously if you are dating someone who lives more than thirty miles away from you. Long-distance relationships are hard to maintain.

1490. There *is* one plus to long-distance romance, though— "Absence makes the heart grow fonder."

1491. If you have dinner plans for an important date, but aren't sure about what to wear, check with the restaurant beforehand.

1492. Always clean your house before having a date over.

1493. The first time you tell someone that you love them, say it in person, not over the phone.

1494. If you get nervous on dates and start to babble, pinch yourself to get a grip on yourself.

1495. If you burn a love letter and the flame is bright, then your love will go smoothly; but if the flame is weak, the relationship will be in trouble—or so the saying goes.

1496. At a party, walk over to a pretty single and say that you have been watching her and like her style.

1497. If you decide to serenade your love interest, go after dark but before 11:00 PM. If you go too late and have to wake her up, it spoils the whole affect.

1498. In a quality relationship you will understand your significant other's opinions, even if they differ from yours.

1499. Start off a romantic date with a ride on an old-fashioned carousel.

1500. If your love interest breaks up with you and states that it's his fault, believe him.

1501. Many singles with parents who were unhappily married secretly fear they, too, will have bad marriages, so they don't date or, if they do, they keep messing things up. If you suffer from this fear, get some counseling. You *can* work through this fear.

1502. When you write a love letter, use beautiful stationery.

1503. Buy an interesting ethnic cookbook and try cooking an exotic dinner together in your kitchen.

1504. Never accept a date for Saturday night after Thursday.

1505. When you write a love letter, make it memorable.

1506. Make your love interest's birthday memorable. Surprise him or her with a bouquet of balloons or a singing telegram.

1507. Tell the truth. It is a lot easier to remember a few dates down the line.

1508. Dressing up for a date is coming back into style all over the country.

1509. Keep in mind that the more love you give away, the more love you will find coming back to you.

1510. The younger the age group, the more likely the couple is to split dating expenses.

1511. Do you want to get to know him better without asking any questions? Have his handwriting analyzed.

Ways to Cheer up after a Bad Date or Break-Up:

1512. Call your mom and tell her about your love-life troubles.

1513. Buy yourself the prettiest bouquet from a street vendor.

1514. Buy yourself that something big that you've always wanted.

1515. Write a letter to a close friend in which you detail precisely what went wrong, in what order, and why. Conclude with a summary that puts the relationship in perspective.

1516. Realize that things might change between the two of you after some time passes.

1517. Send yourself a beautiful plant or bouquet at your office to brighten up your work day.

1518. Buy a huge box of chocolates and indulge yourself.

1519. Throw a big party for yourself. If you don't, who will?

1520. Lose ten pounds and feel great about yourself all over again.

1521. Purchase an outfit that makes you look marvelous.

1522. Go to church this Sunday with your friends.

1523. Read the current bestsellers on the subject of loss.

1524. Take the dream vacation that you always wanted to take, but never got around to taking.

1525. Form a self-help group for others with broken hearts.

1526. Go to a spa for a week and be pampered.

1527. Read the Bible to get your priorities straight.

1528. See a shrink for a healthy, objective point of view on your love life.

1529. Join a singles' support group. There is strength in numbers.

1530. Count your blessings. You still have tons of things to be grateful for.

1531. Realize that break-ups happen to everybody. You aren't the first and you won't be the last.

1532. Bow your head and pray for help.

1533. Make a list of all the things that you didn't like about your significant other. You might end up being glad that he is out of your life!

1534. Remember how great you were feeling before the loss? You will soon feel that way again.

1535. Volunteer to help others who are in worse shape than you.

1536. Write your friends and family letters telling them how much they mean to you—you'll be focusing on the good things in your life instead of the bad.

1537. Get a puppy. You can't be sad with a cute ball of fur following you around the house.

1538. Hug your teddy bear really tight.

1539. Talk to your friends who have been in a situation like this. Find out how they dealt with a broken heart.

1540. Spend the entire day in bed, with the covers pulled up over your head.

1541. Adopt a kitten from the Humane Society. You can't feel too sad when you have just saved a life.

1542. Make a list of ten things that would make you feel better and start doing them. No, you can't seek revenge!

1543. Rent your favorite tearjerker and cry buckets while you watch it. This will help to get the heartache out of your system.

1544. Send a balloon bouquet to yourself on the first week anniversary of the break-up.

1545. Remember the good times in your life before the relationship.

1546. Spend the day with your parents to get a sense of security back into your life.

1547. Make a list of five options you can now pursue that you couldn't before because you were too busy with your ex.

1548. Have a trusted friend remind you of all your good points.

1549. Cry into tissues that are easy on the nose. You don't want to look like Rudolph.

1550. Learn from the mistakes you might have made in the relationship.

1551. Stock up on your favorite junk food and just go hog wild.

1552. Take yourself out to dinner at your favorite restaurant with your best friend.

1553. Get a new hairstyle.

1554. Make a dramatic change in your life— just make sure that it will be a welcome one.

1555. Start an exercise program to start feeling a natural high.

1556. List all the things that are now absent in your life because of this loss and work through each one, one at a time.

1557. Form new friendships that will not remind you of your ex.

1558. Try changing your hair color. If you don't want to make a permanent change, you can get a temporary color done just for fun.

1559. Get a change of scenery. Go on a mini-vacation, stay with a friend, or rearrange your furniture.

1560. Volunteer with Meals on Wheels to deliver meals to home-bound senior citizens. You might make some great older friends.

1561. Lounge at the swimming pool and read a great romance novel.

1562. Clean out your closet and get rid of things, including old love letters.

1563. Don't sit at home and mope.

1564. Clean your house and get rid of any reminders of your old boyfriend/girlfriend.

1565. Beat up your pillow to get rid of your hostility.

1566. Look through old pictures of yourself taken during happier times to remind yourself that you will have great times again.

1567. Treat yourself and a good friend to a long, invigorating hike in the country.

1568. If you don't want to get rid of your memorabilia from this lover, at least box the stuff up and put it out of sight for a little while.

1569. Ask your mom to fix your favorite meal. Moms are always glad to help.

1570. Treat yourself to a great massage.

1571. Hit the beach!

1572. Make fun plans for the upcoming weekend.

1573. Look up an old friend you haven't seen since high school and find out how they're doing.

1574. Surround yourself daily with compassionate, sympathetic friends.

1575. Buy a pair of kooky sunglasses—great for hiding sad eyes.

1576. Dress up in bright, colorful clothes. Even if you don't look happy, your clothes will.

1577. Splurge on a special gift for yourself that your ex wouldn't have thought to buy for you. You can be your own best friend.

1578. Take a long bubble bath or a really hot shower.

1579. Relax in a sauna.

1580. Call old friends you haven't had time to see because of your busy love life.

1581. Decide that your ex is the one who loses out by not having you in his life.

1582. Take a cruise geared for singles.

1583. Find a new hobby to fill your leisure hours.

1584. Take up a new sport. The exercise will do you good.

1585. Redecorate your home or office. Make it a showplace that you will be proud to show to your next significant other.

1586. Consider moving to a cheery, new place that doesn't hold any bad memories for you.

1587. Have a pedicure or a manicure. At least your extremities will be happy!

1588. Find support through the Internet.

1589. Treat yourself to a full-scale make-over. It is time for a change.

1590. Call home often.

1591. Learn not to be afraid of your pain. Face it and work through it.

1592. Do some of your favorite things. Spoil yourself in every way you can think of. You deserve it—big time!

1593. Get fixed up on a blind date. Yes, we want you to get back out there as soon as you feel up to it.

1594. Call someone you have a crush on and just flirt.

1595. Spend a lot of time in the sunshine.

1596. Buy a chic black outfit from a trendy boutique. You never know who will be entering your life today.

1597. Rent your favorite "three-handkerchief" film and have a good old-fashioned cry.

1598. Make a list of all of the things that have gone right in your life up to this point. This will make you focus on the good things, not the loss.

1599. Make a collage of items representing the best times of your life.

1600. Call a friendly former love who can remind you that you are very attractive to members of the opposite sex.

1601. Read a book you have always wanted to read.

1602. Frame a big picture of yourself with a big smile on your face and place it where you can see it every morning.

1603. Use this book to help you find a new love!

1604. After a bad date, give yourself time to feel sad, then move on.

1605. Eat a big banana split.

1606. Lighten up. You will fall in love again!

* * *

Conduct is three-fourths of our life and its largest concern.
—MATTHEW ARNOLD

1607. Don't lose touch with your friends just because you are dating someone.

1608. Keep a smile on your lips. Let the world wonder what you have been up to.

1609. Give your date a penny and tell her that you aren't worth a cent without her.

1610. Risk rejection. Remember the old saying, "No guts, no glory."

1611. Always wear clean, neatly pressed clothes when you go out on a date.

1612. When you are on a date, have manners that would make Emily Post proud.

1613. Primp a little before you leave for a date, even a very casual one.

1614. Dress in a style of clothing that will attract the type of person you want to date.

1615. If you want to stand out in a crowd, wear red.

1616. After a fight, send your significant other a box of Band-Aids to help heal her wounded heart.

1617. Take your love interest ice skating. For maximum romantic value, find a frozen pond or lake and bring some great music along.

1618. Talk your love interest into taking a class with you. That way you will be guaranteed to see her for at least a semester.

1619. Don't wait for a Saturday night to plan a special date. Plan one whenever the mood strikes you.

1620. When you pop the big question, give your fiancée:
The Everything Wedding Etiquette Book
A bride doll
Travel brochures for planning the honeymoon
A wedding planner
A subscription to a bridal magazine
A dozen white roses

1621. If you need to talk over a problem, take a moonlight walk while you talk out your differences.

1622. Subscribe to your local newspaper. It is a dating treasury in which you can find information on all kinds of upcoming events.

1623. If you love children, offer to take a friend's children to the zoo. You might meet an interesting divorced mother or father.

1624. Invest in a book on bartending and learn how to mix drinks for all occasions.

1625. If you learn that your love interest has elderly parents to care for, tread lightly, as he might not want the extra responsibility of a serious relationship.

1626. If you have always wanted to learn a musical instrument, it's never too late to start.

1627. Add a touch of class to your home by starting a collection of beautiful objects, such as bronze or porcelain figurines.

1628. Some singles will stay in a bad relationship because they don't want to go through the hassle and heartache of breaking up. Don't let this happen to you!

1629. Don't put your life on hold for your significant other.

1630. When you serenade your date, take along a beautiful bouquet of flowers.

1631. If you keep running into the same cute single person and you want to get things rolling, tell her that the two of you have to stop meeting like this.

1632. To start a conversation at a big party, ask an attractive single how he knows the host or hostess.

1633. One dating superstition held that if you feel a sharp pain in the chest or the left fourth finger, your lover is being unfaithful.

1634. Make sure that you know your date's plans for the evening so that you are neither overdressed or underdressed.

1635. If you and your love interest come from two different ethnic backgrounds, try to learn as much as you can about your heritages to make sure that you are compatible.

1636. Try an evening of folk dancing at a local church or synagogue. You'll dance with tons of different partners, and it's good exercise too.

1637. You'll feel more attractive and confident if your entire outfit is perfect. Make sure you have attractive and confortable underwear, hosiery, and socks under your nice clothes when on a date.

1638. Stock your bookshelves full of great hardcover books—and read them!

1639. Celebrate payday by asking your love interest out for a fabulous meal at a French restaurant.

1640. Little things mean a lot—send a Hershey Kiss and a Hershey Hug in a tiny box to your significant other when you are out of town and can't be there in person.

1641. If you have a crush on someone, use February 29th as an excuse to ask him out.

1642. Men should always help their dates with their chairs at restaurant tables, in addition to holding doors open.

1643. Before you take the plunge, make sure you have the right partner. Marriage vows are till death do you part. Need we say more?

1644. Relationship stagnation sets in when you get stuck in the "standard date rut." Break out and plan exciting, new activities for upcoming times together.

1645. If she wants an engagement ring for the next upcoming holiday and you aren't ready to give her one, casually tell her in advance that the ring isn't coming at this time to prevent ruining the entire holiday.

1646. When your love interest gets a promotion, tell her that you know she deserved it since her work is first-rate.

1647. If you need to turn down a belligerent suitor, just say "no." Leave it at that.

1648. On your significant other's birthday, take him to lunch and arrange to have a birthday cake served at the restaurant.

1649. When you finally decide to ask your significant other to marry you, make it an unforgettable event.

1650. One of the best things to bring on your dates is a level head. Sometimes you can really need it!

1651. Fun and sexy places to kiss:

Tip of the nose	Temples
Earlobes	Chin
Fingertips	Nape of the neck

1652. Lunch dates are becoming more popular with single parents because the kids are in school and they don't need a sitter.

1653. More and more singles are looking for monogamous relationships instead of playing the field.

1654. Before a date, ask yourself what kind of loving gesture you could make to make the evening extra special.

1655. Let your voice radiate a sense of warmth when you talk to your love interest on the telephone.

1656. Tour a grand historic house with your special someone to marvel at how people lived in past centuries.

1657. Wear a bonnet to church to attract the attention of other singles on Easter.

1658. Be sure to kiss your date at midnight on New Year's Eve.

1659. Take your date to a murder mystery evening at a local restaurant.

Rules for Entertaining Out-of-Town Dates:

1660. Meet your date at the airport—and be on time

1661. Help at the luggage claim by carrying the suitcases.

1662. If you are putting your date up, choose a charming inn or a lovely hotel.

1663. Have a basket of fresh fruit or flowers waiting in the room.

1664. Place a tiny box of chocolates on her pillow.

1665. Provide a schedule of all planned events during her stay.

1666. Ask about her preferences for meals, activities, etc.

1667. Don't put her up at your parents' home unless you are certain she will be welcome there.

1668. Provide her with comfortable transportation. Loan her your car or pick her up, but don't make her wonder how she is going to get around.

1669. Introduce her to your family and friends!

* * *

Three things in human life are important. The first is to be kind. The second is to be kind. The third is to be kind.
—ELBERT HUBBARD

1670. Show off your sleek, new stereo equipment to your date when he drops by. Guys usually love electronics.

1671. Antiques give a home a wonderful, romantic look. Hunt for pieces that have an interesting past, so you can tell your date about each one.

1672. If you and your friends are planning to serenade your love interest, get everyone to dress alike or, at the very least, to dress up.

1673. Most used opening line: "Haven't we met somewhere before?" (You can do better than this!)

1674. Carefully observe how your love interest treats:

Family members	Waiters/waitresses
Friends	Ex-lovers
Animals	Children
Co-workers	Your friends

1675. Think of dating as a growth experience. Yes, some of you have a lot more growing to do than others!

1676. Offer to help your love interest with a major household project.

1677. If you can, get rid of any little habits that drive your significant other up the wall.

1678. Even if you have been together for quite a while, continue to make your times together special.

1679. To feel romantic about your relationship, think of yourself and your lover as a twosome, not as adversaries in the game of love.

1680. If you are making some big decisions, consider their consequences on your significant other and your relationship.

1681. Try to step back and look objectively at your dating relationships.

1682. Try using a fountain pen to write a love letter.

1683. The cardinal rule of writing wonderful love letters is not to censor your deepest emotions.

1684. Women who want an amusing look at the way men think might try reading Dave Barry's *Complete Guide to Guys*.

1685. Never, ever talk about marriage on an early date.

1686. Time heals all broken hearts.

1687. There are cycles in everyone's love life. Learn to endure the dry spells without panicking and to treasure the marvelous moments.

1688. Go to a bookstore and load up on self-help books on romance.

1689. It is true: The best things in life *are* free. Real love doesn't cost a penny.

1690. The three words that every lover longs to hear? "I love you."

1691. Dating trivia: The average first date costs less than thirty-five dollars.

Reasons to Join a Singles' Support Group:

1692. You will make friends with members of both sexes and learn to be comfortable around the opposite sex.

1693. You might just meet the love of your life at a group meeting.

1694. You have nothing to lose by going to a couple of meetings.

1695. It is good to be around a lot of other singles, so you realize you aren't the only one out there.

1696. The people at the meeting will understand what you are facing as a single in today's world.

1697. You can get dating advice from other members.

1698. If you have any questionable dating techniques, you can work on them at the meetings.

1699. You can role-play different dating scenarios with members of the opposite sex.

1700. You will learn how members of the opposite sex view you. This can be a huge eye opener.

1701. Your meetings will be set up on a regular basis, so you can plan what topics to discuss.

1702. At the meetings, you will hear what other singles are experiencing. Trust us, this will make you feel better.

1703. It is a great way to have a bunch of single friends who might just introduce you to the person of your dreams.

1704. After going to a couple of meetings, you will feel much more comfortable with your single status.

1705. These meetings will give you a sense of belonging, which is especially nice when you are not involved in a relationship.

* * *

Speak low, if you speak love.
—*WILLIAM SHAKESPEARE*

1706. Be silly. Send her a box of divinity fudge at work with a note saying that you think she is heavenly.

1707. Pack an elegant picnic basket for an outdoor concert with your special someone.

1708. Talk your love interest into joining your club to make sure you see him on a regular basis.

1709. If you can't get to your love interest across a crowded room, but need to tell her something, use sign language.

1710. Send her an heirloom-quality bride doll to let her know your intentions.

1711. Try a yoga class to relax and improve your flexibility.

1712. Keep a good collection of classical music and maybe even some nature tapes in your car to help set the mood on a date.

1713. Serve a fine bottle of wine when your significant other drops by to share good news with you.

1714. If you have a date coming over for a special dinner, borrow your mother's fine china. You want your table to look gorgeous.

1715. If you are going to a wedding of a close friend, ask her to seat you at the same table as an interesting single man. Many people meet their future spouses at weddings—you can't ask for a more romantic atmosphere!

1716. Dating superstition: If you want to know your future, hold up a holly leaf and with each point of the leaf declare, "Daughter, wife, widow, nun." When you touch the last point, you will know your fate.

1717. On your next dinner date, hold up your glass in a grand gesture and make a romantic toast to your love interest.

1718. If you and your significant other have major economic differences, talk about them before you tie the knot.

1719. If you meet an attractive stranger and she is wearing a ring on her fourth finger of her left hand that doesn't look like a traditional diamond engagement ring, ask her if the ring is in fact an engagement ring. You have nothing to lose and everything to gain.

How to Evaluate Your Current Romantic Relationship:

1720. Listen to your heart. What is it telling you?

1721. What do your friends think of the two of you as a couple?

1722. Are you having a lot more good times than bad times in the relationship?

1723. Are your relationship goals the same as your love interest's?

1724. What does your family think? What does your love interest's family think?

1725. Are you happy? Are you glad that you are involved with this person?

* * *

Kiss the tear from her lip,
you'll find the rose the sweeter for the dew.
—*JOHN WEBSTER*

1726. Get to know your new love interest's:
Birthday   Favorite movie
Hobbies   Favorite music
Occupation

1727. When you know that your significant other is wearing something new, comment on it.

1728. With most couples, the person who is more financially secure pays for most of the dates.

1729. Change your usual clothing style to get noticed by members of the opposite sex who see you often.

1730. Wear a fabulous cologne as your own personal trademark.

1731. For men only: Volunteer your services at a local bachelor auction for charity. You'll have fun when women bid on you, and the winning bidder could be your dream date.

1732. The way to the heart is through the tummy so, when all else fails, bake chocolate chip cookies. The recipe on the bag of chips is tried and true. Bring them to your love interest in a pretty basket.

1733. Get involved in your local community group. Speak up at meetings on issues that interest you.

1734. While on vacation, send postcards to anyone you are interested in. It is a great excuse to say hello.

1735. Do ordinary things in extraordinary ways.

1736. Visit an out-of-state relative for a change of scene. They might even know someone interesting for you to meet.

1737. Reasons people date:
For fun and romance
For companionship
To find a mate

1738. Cultivate an aura of romance about you.

1739. When you tease a date, know when to stop. You want to end it while you are both still laughing.

1740. How you see yourself will greatly influence how others see you.

1741. Stop yourself from asking your date's:
Annual income   Rent payment
Price of home   Savings account balance

Into Each Romance Some Rain Must Fall, or How to Argue Constructively:

1742. Remain calm, especially if this is your first fight.

1743. Fight about one topic at a time and be specific about what the problem is.

1744. Pick a time to talk that is good for both of you. You don't want to be tired or rushed.

1745. Tell your side of the story in a positive manner. Refrain from putting down your significant other.

1746. Listen to your love interest's side of the story. Remember that every argument has two sides.

1747. Be open and honest. If you are wrong, admit it.

1748. Once you end the disagreement, kiss each other and forget about it.

* * *

Chide a friend in private and praise him in public.
—SOLON

Key Events on the Road to Becoming a Couple:

1749. You meet each other's friends.

1750. You meet each other's family.

1751. You work together on a home maintenance project.

1752. You give each other a tour of your work places.

1753. You make a significant purchase of some kind together.

1754. You begin to entertain as a couple.

* * *

Over two thousand weddings are performed in Las Vegas on Valentine's Day each year. The second busiest day for the city's thirty-five wedding chapels is New Year's Eve.

1755. Read *2002 Things to Do on a Date* to get ideas for unique and exciting alternatives to the dreaded "standard date rut."

1756. Make a time capsule of your relationship as soon as you become engaged. You might want to include:
　　Newspapers and magazines
　　Buttons from political campaigns
　　Ticket stubs from events you attended as a couple
　　Car, real estate, and grocery store ads
　　Movies guides
　　Relationship memorabilia
　　Open the capsule on your tenth anniversary.

1757. Adaptability is a great virtue to have when you are dating.

1758. Be self-sufficient on your dates. Don't expect your love interest to entertain you. Be the type of person who can entertain himself.

1759. It is true that birds of a feather flock together. What does his choice of friends tell you about his personality?

1760. Don't make up excuses for your date's poor behavior.

1761. Are you being shallow? You might be if you are judging your dates strictly on their:
Bank account	Good looks
Social position	Occupation
Designer clothing	Luxury car
Jewelry	Home

1762. If an acquaintance wants to set you up on a blind date, find out what his motives are. Is he a good Samaritan, a busybody, or simply a friend of a desperate single?

1763. If you are meeting a cute stranger for the very first time and you are interested in him, give his hand an extra little squeeze when you shake it.

1764. If you spot a pretty single in a bar, send over a drink with a note written on a napkin to join you.

1765. Bring your date a flower (we recommend a long-stemmed pink one).

1766. If you want to win a place in your love interest's heart, offer to help him this weekend with a chore around his house.

1767. Clip an item in your newspaper that you know he would find interesting.

1768. Touch your love interest lightly while involved in a serious conversation. You want to feel connected to each other.

1769. Try batting your eyes at him while having a drink in a dark bar.

1770. Tease her about her good looks.

1771. If you know his schedule, "bump" into him and suggest going out for a cup of coffee.

1772. Offer to put up her bookshelves or hang her curtains.

1773. Take note of any "sensitive spots" your date has and stay clear of them when teasing him.

1774. To get into a romantic frame of mind, read poetry by W. B. Yeats, Robert Graves, John Clare, Sir Walter Raleigh, Edmund Waller, John Fletcher, Elizabeth Jennings, John Donne, and A. D. Hope.

1775. Stormy weather or the final stages of a relationship is marked by:

Shock	Denial
Anger	Heartache
Acceptance	Moving on and loving again

1776. Get your name in the social columns on a regular basis.

1777. Becoming a leader in community affairs enables you to meet lots of great singles.

1778. Take some dance lessons. You'll shine on the dance floor!

1779. Get your photograph in your company's newsletter when you get a promotion.

1780. Be your own press agent and spread positive stories about yourself.

1781. Get listed in *Who's Who* if you want to impress your date.

1782. Enter radio call-in contests that singles might be listening to.

1783. Be a high-energy, enthusiastic person. You will attract more people this way.

1784. Here's our list of "Most Romantic Things":
    Foreign city—Paris
    U.S. city—Carmel, Calif.
    Flower—Red rose
    Poet—Elizabeth Barrett Browning
    Song—"Unforgettable"
    Month—June (for all the June brides)
    Season—Spring
    Holiday—A tie between New Year's Eve and
        Valentine's Day
    Drink—Champagne
    Book—*2002 Ways To Say, "I Love You"*
    Jewel—Diamond
    Question—"Will you marry me?"

1785. If you want to meet professionals, travel business class whenever you fly.

1786. Carry a book with an unusual title to use as a conversation starter. We suggest *2002 Things to Do on a Date*.

1787. Learn to speak up and introduce yourself to people everywhere you go.

1788. Help all strangers in distress.

1789. Become an authority on a certain topic and give lectures whenever you get the chance. You never know who will be in the audience.

1790. Our choice for one of the most romantic of all dates:
    Begin with a drink at a trendy wine bar
    Have dinner at a French restaurant
    Take a horse-drawn carriage ride
    Stop for a nightcap at an out-of-the way cafe

1791. If you want to have dates coming out of the woodwork, become a contestant in a beauty pageant.

1792. Trade in your old reliable car for a flashy, new sports car.

1793. Take sailing lessons for a chance at love on the high seas.

1794. On a rainy day carry a large umbrella and offer to share it with a cute stranger who isn't as well prepared for the weather as you are.

1795. When you attend seminars, ask intelligent questions. You want to get the attention of any interesting people that are there.

1796. Practice having good posture.

1797. If you know you truly love your love interest and that you always want to be with her, propose! What are you waiting for?

1798. Place a happy ad in the classifieds on your love interest's birthday or on a big dating anniversary.

1799. Try writing a romantic poem or song about your significant other.

1800. Ask your date early for an important event, so she doesn't think she is your second choice.

1801. You don't have to go out for every date. Try a game of chess or Monopoly on a cold winter's night.

1802. If your love interest gets a new hairstyle, be sure to compliment her on it.

Three-fourths of the people you will meet tomorrow are hungering and thirsting for sympathy. Give it to them, and they will love you.
—DALE CARNEGIE

1803. When you hear that one of your love interest's friends is in the hospital, plan to visit the person together.

1804. To have fresh breath, use mouthwash before you go out on a date.

1805. When you meet your love interest's pampered pooch, be sure to say something nice about it.

1806. Offer to help your cute co-worker with a project.

1807. Want more romance in your life? Paint your living room a deep red to give your home a feeling of warmth.

1808. Use the term that's right for your serious relationship:
Going steady   Boyfriend/Girlfriend
An item   Pre-engagement
Exclusive relationship

1809. If you don't like to iron your clothes, send them to the cleaners to be pressed. You don't want to look like an unmade bed, do you?

1810. Offer to baby-sit your love interest's children to win brownie points.

1811. Alternate planning dating activities. You plan this week's date and your significant other plans next week's.

1812. Treat your mate as a person, not as a thing.

1813. Drive out to a gorgeous nature park and have a picnic.

1814. Treat your significant other as if he was the most important person in the world.

1815. For guys only: Don't promise to call at the end of a date if you know you never will.

1816. In a bar, turn to a good-looking stranger and ask what she is drinking.

1817. Take a little gift, instead of flowers, to your date.

1818. Say hello with a hug.

1819. Plan a romantic weekend away from home for just the two of you.

1820. If your new love interest won't let you call him at home, he could be married.

1821. Make him homemade chicken soup when he has a cold.

1822. Always listen to your "gut" feelings.

1823. During tough times in your relationship, use positive, supportive words when you talk over problems. Negative, hurtful words will only add to your problems.

1824. Buy him a cute little windup toy to keep on his desk at work.

1825. To see your love interest clearly, write out a detailed description of her without editing your thoughts. Read it a few days later and read between the lines. Do you like the person you have described?

1826. If you ask people for dating advice, be open and listen to it. Don't be defensive.

1827. Listen to National Public Radio for interesting anecdotes to tell to your love interest.

1828. Never cheat; we repeat, never cheat!

1829. Don't try to please every single member of the opposite sex.

1830. Plan for your engagement to last at least six months. Research shows that longer engagements are better for couples than shorter ones.

1831. Want to be a great mate? Give without the expectation of getting in return.

1832. Be advised: Weddings usually take a long time to plan.

1833. If your love interest invites you to her party, offer to help her with it.

1834. A VCR is a good dating investment because you can always invite a date over in the middle of the week to see a great movie.

1835. True love can take a long time to grow; learn to be patient.

1836. Guys: On a cold night, give her your jacket.

1837. The most romantic gifts for her:
Pearls   Tickets to the ballet
Perfume   A handmade quilt
A teddy bear   A leather-bound edition of
A gold bracelet   her favorite classic novel
A diamond engagement ring

1838. When you plan to stay at your significant other's parents' home, find out the "rules" of the house before you visit.

1839. Love cannot be bought (unless you get a puppy), so don't try to impress your date with extravagant gifts early in the relationship. Save them till they are truly an expression of love.

1840. If you like your date's choice of friends, tell her.

1841. Before you let a friend set you up on a blind date, get a detailed description of the person.

1842. Ask your opposite-sex parent for his/her take on your love life.

1843. Many men prefer women to wear skirts instead of pants.

A kiss is a lovely trick designed by nature to stop speech when words become superfluous.
—INGRID BERGMAN

1844. Need a dose of positive thinking? Read books by Norman Vincent Peale.

1845. Young lovers take heed: Most states require parental permission for those under eighteen years of age to get married.

1846. Before you go out to dinner with your love interest's family, learn something about them to make you feel more comfortable.

1847. Having a date over for dinner? Try making homemade pizza together.

1848. When your date takes you out to dinner, be kind and don't order the most expensive item on the menu.

1849. If your love interest invites you to her party, be sure and tell her at the end of the night that it was a great success.

1850. If you invite your love interest over for dinner and you burn it, relax and order in.

1851. After a painful break-up, stay away from your "perfect couple" friends for at least a week or two. You can talk to them on the phone, but save yourself some heartache by not seeing them in person until you feel better about your love life.

1852. Learn to speak a romantic foreign language, such as French or Italian.

1853. Only date singles who are supportive of your career.

1854. When you meet someone terrific, focus on the moment, not on what the other person might be thinking about you.

1855. Are you ready to give an engagement ring? Give her it in an elegant box that she will treasure almost as much as the ring.

1856. If you decide to break off a long-term relationship, have a meeting with your significant other to discuss the break-up, so that both of you will have a sense of closure. This will make it easier for both of you to move forward.

1857. When you meet your love interest's family, be sure to say positive things about them to your love interest afterwards.

1858. Want to spark a romance with a friend? Try a romantic activity together, like going out dancing or a moonlight picnic.

1859. Buy her a really special Christmas ornament. You could be hanging it on your tree next year as a married couple.

1860. On a crowded bus, give an attractive woman your seat.

1861. Buy some dog treats or catnip for your love interest's furry friend.

1862. Join a local environmental volunteer clean-up project.

1863. Sign up for a canoe trip through the Sierra Club or your local park or nature center.

1864. Carry a camera and ask a good-looking stranger to take your picture in front of a local tourist spot. Strike up a conversation from there.

1865. Arrange to have the engagement ring on her dessert plate during that special proposal dinner.

1866. If you have a crush on a waiter/waitress, try:
    Going to the restaurant often
    Leaving a big tip
    Sitting at his or her tables only

1867. If you would like to meet someone in your field, send your business card in the mail with an invitation to lunch to discuss your work.

1868. If you go to bars, keep your eyes peeled for wedding band tan lines on the fourth finger on the left hand if you suspect that an attractive stranger might be married.

1869. Too much togetherness can spoil even the best of romances.

1870. Want to express your feelings, but you're not ready to use the L-word? Just tell your love interest that you care for them a great deal and leave it at that.

1871. If your current flame mentions a favorite meal or snack, offer to fix it or cook it together.

1872. Buy a new dress or suit to make you feel more excited about a big dinner date.

1873. In most age groups, there are more women than men. Ladies, take heart: Just look smarter, not harder for love.

1874. Eventually even the most die-hard singles get tired of dating and want to settle down. Is your love interest worth the wait?

1875. When you go over to your date's home, compliment him on it.

1876. Most single men don't have many Christmas decorations. Offer to share yours.

1877. In a crowded restaurant during the lunch hour rush, offer to share your table with an attractive single person.

1878. If you have a fight with your significant other, don't make one of you into a winner and the other into a loser.

1879. Don't think of marriage as the answer to all your problems. If you don't marry the right person, it could be the beginning of even more troubles.

1880. If your date didn't like you, accept that fact that some people just don't hit it off.

1881. Never tell someone you are in love until you are.

1882. Put away pictures of your exes, at least temporarily, so that your new significant other won't feel bad.

1883. If you shake hands during an introduction, be sure that you have a nice, firm grip.

1884. When you have your date over for dinner, borrow your grandmother's sterling flatware to set a beautiful table.

1885. At a nightclub, ask the band to dedicate a song to your significant other.

1886. If you want to make a dance special, ask the band to play "your song."

1887. Treat yourself to a relaxing facial to improve your skin. Both men and women can enjoy these.

1888. Express your appreciation when your date plans an extra-special evening out on the town.

1889. When you go to your love interest's parents' home for the first time, you might want to dress more conservatively than you usually do.

1890. Some of the best dates are made on the spur of the moment. Learn to be spontaneous—you will have a lot more fun.

1891. Trust is one of the most important bonds between a man and a woman.

1892. Our picks for great early dates:
Dog or cat shows   Country auctions
Blockbuster movies   Museum exhibits
Brunch at a new restaurant
A Saturday morning game of tennis or golf

1893. Act like an adult when things don't go your way on a date.

1894. Great gifts for birthdays, when you have dated each other less than six weeks:
Current bestseller   Computer games
Homemade goodies   Balloon bouquet
Gourmet food   Flowers

1895. Want to get attention at work? Have your parents send you flowers.

1896. Use some room fragrance or potpourri to set the mood in your home before a big date.

1897. Give your significant other's pooch holiday gifts.

1898. Enjoy being you!

1899. Want to impress your date? Toast her with crystal champagne glasses.

Love those who love you.

—VOLTAIRE

1900. When you toast your date, say what's in your heart.

1901. As you go about your daily life, walk with a sense of purpose.

1902. Singles really check each other out at a swimming pool. Be sure that your swimsuit is flattering.

1903. If you want to see your date again, try to make plans for another date before the evening ends.

1904. When you are meeting a date, take along her phone number just in case she doesn't show up. You can always call and find out if there was a mix-up in the plans.

1905. If you mess up on a date, send a little note asking your love interest to forgive you.

1906. Learn from your dating fiascoes; don't keep repeating them.

1907. Before you go on a date, check to make sure you have your date's correct address.

1908. Try to find that tricky balance between autonomy and intimacy in your romantic relationships.

1909. Stop trying to change your boyfriends/girlfriends. You can only change yourself.

1910. Sign up for a gourmet cooking class and impress her by cooking her a delicious meal.

He who sedulously attends, pointedly asks, calmly speaks, coolly answers, and ceases when he has no more to say, is in possession of some of the best requisites of man.

—JOHANN KASPAR LAVATER

1911. Think up absurd pet names for each other that you would never reveal to other people.

1912. Never make a commitment before you are 100 percent ready to do so.

1913. If you call your love interest at work, keep the conversation brief.

1914. Tell yourself every "single" day that you are a fabulous person and anyone would be glad to be dating you.

1915. The road to true love is seldom a straight one.

1916. If your love life isn't the one of your dreams, be bold and start making the necessary changes to get your life in line with your dreams. It can be done!

1917. Ninety-eight percent of the U. S. population gets married by the age of forty. Relax, the odds are in your favor.

1918. Age doesn't make any difference—*everyone* wants to have a romantic relationship.

1920. Sometimes the old saying is true: Love *is* better the second time around.

1921. People often reveal a great deal about themselves on early dates. Listen carefully. Because your date doesn't know you well enough to screen what he says, you might hear some very eye-opening statements. Sometimes these tidbits are great news, and other times they are huge red flags that tell you to move on.

1922. If you aren't looking for a long-term commitment, but your love interest is, speak up.

1923. Make sure that you see your love interest under all kinds of circumstances to get a better idea of what the person is really like. Watch them:

At work	With children
When sick	When tired
Under stress	After a hard day

1924. If you want to give your love interest an ego boost, display her picture on your desk at the office.

1925. Be romantic and keep track of all dating anniversaries:

When you met	First telephone call
First date	First kiss
When you fell in love	

1926. If your date suggests an activity that isn't for you, don't turn down the date, just suggest another activity.

1927. If you are a die-hard smoker, don't light up until you know if your date is allergic to or bothered by smoke.

1928. Always touch up your makeup in the ladies room, not in front of your date.

1929. If the two of you are of different religions, try attending each other's houses of worship together.

1930. Sudden, wild romances usually end the same way!

1931. Nothing beats love at first sight except love with insight.

1932. Refuse to enter into a competitive relationship with your love interest.

1933. Send your new love interest a fun, romantic e-mail. Use code names if others might see it.

1934. Keep in mind that you can give without loving, but you can't love without giving.

1935. You want to be someone's date, not his therapist. If you are constantly solving one crisis after another, consider finding him a therapist or a self-help group.

1936. Use your license plate to hunt for love. Get a plate that says, "B-Mine" or another fun saying.

1937. The all-time worst line: "I love you too much to marry you."

1938. Knit him a scarf or sweater. He'll remember you every time he puts it on.

1939. It is a sad fact: Love quickens everyone's senses—except common sense.

1940. If you are in love with each other, but have a serious problem that you can't seem to work out, see a therapist together.

1941. If your current love interest has a habit of canceling dates at the last minute, consider canceling the relationship.

1942. After a break-up, don't let your friends or your ex's friends fill you in on his current love life status.

1943. To keep a relationship from getting stale, have a regular G.N.O./B.N.O. (girls' night out/boys' night out) in your hectic schedule.

1944. After a break-up, try not to run into your ex for at least a month. This will give your heart some time to mend.

1945. Kiss your date the way you like to be kissed.

1946. Collect your favorite inspirational verses on love and romance. Record them on a tape recorder in your own voice and play the tape several times a week at night before you go to sleep.

1947. Gently tell a bad kisser the way that you like to be kissed. Make the conversation short and upbeat. Then demonstrate.

1948. Don't confuse looking for the perfect mate with looking for the right mate. No one is perfect and if you wait for the perfect person to come along, you'll spend the rest of your life alone.

1949. A great love affair needs plenty of LSD—love, security, and diamonds.

1950. When he gives you a diamond engagement ring, give him an engagement gift such as a gold watch, gold cuff links, or a fine leather Bible with the date of your engagement inscribed on it.

1951. Hide an engagement ring:

In a heart-shaped box   On a Christmas tree
In an ice cube   On a teddy bear
In a bouquet of roses   On a dog's collar
In a box of Godiva chocolates
In a cake with the proposal written in icing on the top

1952. Our picks for romantic dates:

Dancing
A sleigh ride in the snow
A gourmet picnic under the stars
A glass of brandy in front of a roaring fire on a
   cold winter's night

1953. It is wonderful to make loving gestures with cards, flowers, and the like, but don't continue making them if your love interest doesn't reciprocate.

1954. Be wary of lovers who try to buy your affection with gifts.

1955. If your date hurts your feelings, tell him right away. Don't sit and sulk for the rest of the date.

1956. If your date stands you up without a valid reason, never accept another date with this person.

1957. Never act incompetent to boost your date's ego.

1958. When you and your significant other finally get around to talking about past relationships, be very cautious. It is better to say too little, than to regret saying too much.

1959. A great rule to follow in matters of the heart is: If someone hurts you once, shame on them; if someone hurts you twice, shame on you for letting them.

1960. In the dating world, timing is everything. You may meet someone and be attracted to him, but find he is dating someone else. Then he breaks up with them, but now *you* are dating someone else. Never burn your bridges, however. You might both end up available at the same time.

1961. Spend some time objectively looking at your love interest.

1962. Ask your married friends for their advice on your love life. They will have a different perspective than your single friends. It is good to listen to both sides.

1963. Use your married friends as role models if they are living the love life of your dreams. Watch them and learn.

1964. When the heart is ready, the lover will appear.

1965. Be smart about your love life. Take it seriously. After all, you are looking at making a lifetime commitment.

1966. When your friends get married, don't give up your friendships with them.

1967. Ask your married friends to fix you up on blind dates. Most married couples enjoy being involved again in the dating world.

1968. Rate your date. How did he or she measure up in areas like:
Level of fun	Romance
Chemistry	Manners
Appearance	Thoughtfulness

1969. To be your best, take care of yourself body, mind, and soul.

1970. Learn to express your wants and needs to your significant other in a non-threatening way.

1971. Even if you are planning to pay cash on a date, carry a credit card in case the evening is more expensive than you had planned.

1972. Be as loyal to a date as you would be to a friend.

1973. We hope you know that romantic love usually does not conquer all.

1974. Be nice to your date's family, friends, co-workers, neighbors, and pets. Their opinions about you can make a big difference in how your date thinks of you.

1975. Shop for gifts in advance, so you'll come up with wonderful presents.

1976. Show that you care by bringing up subjects that she talked about on previous dates.

1977. Are you too scared to propose in person? Then try:
Placing your proposal in a window display
Hiring a skywriter to pop the big question
Asking her on a billboard

1978. If you feel uncomfortable with a date's question, just ignore it or say that you'd rather not answer. Never divulge more about yourself than you are comfortable in doing.

1979. Treat every single date the way you would like to be treated. Yes, every one of them!

1980. Never keep a date waiting while you try to decide what to wear. Plan your wardrobe in advance.

1981. The most popular places to meet are:

Church	School
Work	Bars
Coffeehouses	Friends' homes
Supermarkets	Weddings

1982. Don't punish your significant other for a mistake. Use it as a growth experience.

1983. Talk about your relationship at least every other week to make sure it is running smoothly. A lot of relationships die because of little problems which, left unaddressed, grow way out of proportion.

1984. Keep in mind that men and women see things *very* differently. Make concessions for those differences.

1985. Exchange lists with your significant other of ways to improve your relationship to make it even more wonderful.

1986. Never do the same thing on a date twice in a row. Variety is the spice of life.

1987. Always be yourself; otherwise you create credibility problems with your dates.

1988. Looking for a doctor? (Your mother is.) The ten states with the highest percentages of physicians per capita:

Hawaii	Washington, D.C.
Massachusetts	Maryland
Connecticut	Rhode Island
New Jersey	California
Vermont	New York

1989. If your families' and friends' opinions differ greatly from yours on your love interest, take a second look. Often, they can see more clearly because they can be objective.

1990. Look at your love interest's reputation carefully. It will tell you a great deal about his character.

1991. Sometimes singles get so nervous on a first date that they say something totally out of character. If you feel anything positive at all for your date, give him a second chance.

1992. Use your imagination when deciding what to do on a date. Planning a good date means you are halfway to having a great time.

1993. Very few people have met their Mr./Miss Right without having a broken heart or two along the way.

1994. Learn to view the single statistics in your favor. For example, if your city has 20,000 single men and 10,000 single women, don't view this negatively if you are a man. Rejoice that you have 10,000 women to choose from.

1995. Listen very closely to what your date tells you of his hopes and dreams. If they aren't compatible with yours, move on.

1996. The key phrases of all long-term relationships are:

I'm sorry.	You were right.
I love you.	I was wrong.
Thank you.	Will you marry me?

1997. Try to discern if your love interest is a modern or traditional type of person and then plan your dating strategy accordingly.

1998. With some people you click immediately, with others it can take a long time. Never close a door until you are absolutely positive that your relationship wouldn't work.

1999. If you feel you need an excuse to ask out your new love interest, but don't have one, try one of these unusual occasions:
> The night of a new moon rising
> The Chinese New Year
> National Anthem Day (March 3)
> Easter Even (Saturday before Easter)
> The anniversary of baseball's perfect game (May 5)
> Kiss and Make Up Day (August 25)
> Double Tenth Day (October 10)
> Sandwich Day (November 3)
> Underdog Day (December 15)

2000. Read *2002 Ways to Say "I Love You"* to get creative ideas on expressing your romantic feelings to your significant other.

2001. Wonderful places to propose:
> In the middle of a beautiful woods in the fall of the year
> At a quaint cabin up in the mountains
> During dinner at a four-star restaurant
> During the half-time celebrations at a ball game
> In front of a roaring fireplace during the Christmas holidays
> At a scenic old mill
> While browsing among the masterpieces at a museum
> On a boat pier at sunset
> While dining at a charming, country inn

2002. Remember that every single pot has a lid, so live happy, happily ever after!

My most brilliant achievement was my ability to be able to persuade my wife to marry me.
>   —*WINSTON CHURCHILL*
